A Contradiction of Terms:
A 25th Division Analyst's Tour in Vietnam, April 1970 to March 1971

Joseph C. Maguire Jr.

2021

To Margie Ann Bonnett
Best wishes
Joe Maguire
April 18, 2024

Copyright © 2021 by Joseph C. Maguire Jr.

All rights reserved.

To Clinton Angelo Fields, Private, USMC

Clinton was a classmate of mine at Mergenthaler High School, in Baltimore. We called him "Sugar Bear". He preceded me to Vietnam by three years and died in the service of his country within a few months of his arrival.

I also dedicate this to his mother, Elenor Fields, whom I met at the dedication of the Maryland Vietnam Veterans Memorial in 1989. I wanted her to know that he will always be remembered.

ACKNOWLEDGEMENTS

Impleting this, I have some people to thank for their understanding, time and patience. Each person involved in this brought with them their unique combination of talents, as well as another set of eyes, which were invaluable, when I couldn't see the forest for the trees. Whenever I felt that I was wasting my time on this, there was always someone to remind me of how important it was for me to write this.

Over the years, since I had my first thoughts of writing about Vietnam I have interacted with many people; some were teachers of various disciplines, others I worked with as a matter of circumstance, and some were family.

Other individuals having more spirit than technical ability urged me on, while others who were indifferent or even totally against the effort, for various reasons, felt that I should leave it alone. This resistance served yet another reason to carry on. I am glad that I didn't take the latter's advice.

Certain professors at the University of Baltimore influenced my project in the formative stages. Drs. D. Randall Bierne Thomas Jacklin, Ben Primer, and George Klein were helpful just by offering their varying philosophies of History, and the practical means of conveying it.

Doctors Bierne and Jacklin, both with The University of Baltimore faculty and Johns Hopkins alumni, represented opposite ends of the spectrum of public opinion concerning the war. I have always appreciated their candor. Probably the best way that I can thank them is to apply what I've learned in my association with them while at the University and afterward.

The people who read the various segments or discussed the project with me, even if only to draw parallels to their own experience, have my special thanks. I very much appreciate their taking the time to give me the benefit of their diverse writing talents, as well as their feelings on the subject.

Anita Aidt Guy, a Maryland historian and professor at the College of Notre Dame of Maryland and a doctoral graduate of Georgetown University, generously took time from her own projects and her teaching to look over various segments of my work and offered helpful suggestions.

Virginia North, archivist of Maryland's Jewish Historical Society- formerly of the Maryland Historical Society, has known of this project since I started putting this in manuscript form, in the mid-nineteen eighties. One of her Goucher coursework papers involved me as an interviewee and prompted some questions that I could answer better with continuing my own project.

Eileen Rudert, of the Civil Rights Commission, another Hopkins graduate and former Maryland Historical Society volunteer was another wonderful advisor. Her area of expertise involved technical writing, and I will always appreciate her attempts to educate me in those aspects.

Dr. Robert Bruger, also of the Maryland Historical Society, has looked at the various segments of the work, and offered some suggestions. His experience with the Marine Corps in Vietnam was a striking mix of parallels and contrasts, to mine. He was also quite helpful in showing me what was already been written about the Vietnam War.

In the late 1980's, The National Archives released some records of the units that were involved in Vietnam operations. The overall project to organize and classify these documents scheduled to for completion in the mid-1990's; some records were available, at this time. Fortunately, the information concerning the 25th Infantry Division was one of the first record groups made available. Rich Boylan and his staff in the Military Records section of Archives Annex in Suitland were most helpful in showing what was available. On one occasion, Rich took me downstairs to show us what he was up against in making these records available to the public. It looked like the closing scene of <u>Raiders of the Lost Ark</u>, in which the Ark of the Covenant was lost in a sea of crates, in an incredibly huge storage area. He related the story about those records warehoused in Long Binh until April of 1975 and how close they came to be the property of the North Vietnamese. Records of some of the more active units were, as of that time still not located. Rich was still looking for records of his unit, in the 199th Light Infantry Brigade. Perhaps, they were just misplaced and eventually found. I thank Rich and his staff for their help over that time and hope to return the favor someday with a project more directly related to the use of this immense record group.

Most of all, I thank my family, who in various ways gave me the reasons for writing this book: my sister, Sharon Bryant, my brother Pat, my daughter, Linda, my son Joseph and especially my wife, Betty. No one could have such a supportive wife. She had to live this all over again. She saved every letter that I sent home, was my primary contact when I was in Vietnam and was as much of a participant as anyone could have been without being there. I will always love her. Her comments on the transcript were a constant reminder that I was on the right path and that what I did counted.

In recent years Jan Herman and David Truscello gave feedback to the manuscript when I couldn't objectively look at it anymore.

Because of their efforts on my behalf, they have reminded me what this is about- it's was more than a war and it's not something that could be isolated from the National scene. Jan and David have never met. Their views, however, have proved invaluable and have guided a critical focus of this writing.

Jan Was a Vietnam Era veteran. He has been associated with the Naval Institute. He has written and reviewed many articles and books. One of his books was a description of events surrounding the U.S.S. Kirk and its role in the evacuation of Vietnamese nationals at the end of the war. I met Jan at an event, sponsored by PBS, commemorating a welcoming home for Vietnam veterans at Timonium Fairgrounds, near Baltimore. One of his functions there was to encourage writers, like myself, to add their particular focus to the Vietnam experience. He looked at my manuscript and offered many helpful suggestions. Thanks, Jan!

David is a retired professor who taught English, Cultural Awareness and related subjects at Community College of Baltimore County for about thirty-five years. He was the English coordinator, at one point. As an adjunct professor in that department, I had many opportunities, during my time at CCBC, to talk with him on a wide range of subjects. He provided yet other dimensions to this with his own circumstantial involvement in the events. David was in school, at Kent State, during the events of May 1970. He experienced, first-hand and, in whole other ways, how these events affected our country. I assisted him in his retirement presentation, which illustrated these contrasts, similarities, and connections to those times. I was honored to be part of it. His input on my project has been most meaningful and heartfelt. I can't thank him enough. All the best, my friend!

CONTENTS

PREFACE x
INTRODUCTION 1

PART I- PRE VIETNAM

HOME 8
SPRING 1969 14
FORT BRAGG 23
FORT HOLABIRD 29
 HOLABIRD CONTINUED 48
OAKLAND 51
VIETNAM-BOUND 55

PART II- CU CHI BASECAMP

ARRIVAL 59
CU CHI BASECAMP 63
25TH MIC 68
OB 72
TRANSIENT HOOTCH 74
JUNGLE TRAINING 77
CAMBODIAN OPERATIONS 83
LIFE ON CU CHI BASECAMP 92
WEATHER 102

RELIGIOUS SERVICES	105
DETAILS	106
BUNKER GUARD	109
DAY WORKERS	115
25th MIC PERSONALITIES	119
OTHER PERSONALITIES	128
HOME EVENTS	132
CU CHI SUMMARY	141

PART III- XUAN LOC

THE JOURNEY	144
XUAN LOC PERSONALITIES	152
XUAN LOC ROUTINE	158
2/25TH DIVISION OPERATIONS	161
ALERT	166
A CHRISTMAS IN VIETNAM	173
WINTER IN XUAN LOC	181
SIDE TRIPS	188
REALIZATIONS	193
HOI CHAN	196
XUAN LOC MENANGERIE	200
2/25'S LAST XUAN LOC OPERATIONS	205
XUAN LOC FAREWELL	210

PART IV- LONG BINH AND HOME

CAMP FRENZEL-JONES	221
FRENZEL-JONES PERSONALITIES	225
DIVERSIONS	228
LAST OPERATIONS	232
...ON MY WAY BACK HOME	235

REPLACEMENT DEPOT	241
EPILOGUE	247
Bibliographies	258
Bibliographic Sources: National Archives	258
Bibliographic Sources- Books	264
Index	267

PREFACE

It has been over fifty years since my leaving for Vietnam. This may be an opportune time to assess this and wrap up my present writing project. There are many other things to write about, but this has been one of the most pervasive subjects to deal with and an impetus for gathering and developing the various skills necessary for pursuing all sorts of writing and research.

My insights are limited to specific areas of my location, job classification and any life experiences that or insights gathered along the way. In research. One compositional constant is to narrow the topic. Following this, I can address how this complex matter manifested itself through me.

American involvement in Vietnam is obviously complex and any attempt to explain it fully, in simplistic terms is inadequate. The topic can be approached through a variety of filters. My filter is to report it as I saw, felt and realized along the way.

In this topic-narrowing, I spent a lot of time trying to examine and resolve what had happened, historically, politically, socially and personally- attempting to wrap it into one bundle and putting it out there to interpret what happened. This is the result.

My focus was continually being influenced by more information and, subsequently more revelation, as I was living these things and my objectivity was constantly challenged. When I started this, there was little to work with. The War and it's after-affects were too prevalent to effectively address.

This is where a constant assessment of my values and of my true purpose are at issue.

What does it mean? Why should it still mean anything, in observing how others in my direct experience were handling this, a whole range of possibilities emerged, ranging from spilling everything I know (which wouldn't take long and wouldn't be too prudent) to blocking it out entirely and starting fresh (with its own hazards, including amnesia, and previous enculturation).

The resolution, as with all writing, is to go for the truth in how I handle these things. When what I write feels right, I can accept another point of view, judge it for its relevance and move on, hopefully learning all the time. To enhance its effectiveness. If I find a useful insight along the way, I'd like to share it and everyone will be better for it.

Seeking agreement with my result is not my intended goal. Having something to share and adding to the dialogue is. There has got to be a teaching moment no matter how subtle and if I can help toward that, I've done what I've started out to do from the beginning.

INTRODUCTION

On matters pertaining to Vietnam, I've collected a number of letters, printed orders, manuals, photographs, pamphlets, books, audio tapes and handwritten items for the project, in my effort to piece things together. It's no coincidence that my letters to Betty from April 1970 to March 1971 were major resources for starting this work. An examination of those letters, alone, would be a noteworthy project, in many ways. On one level, it shows my feelings about missing home, and my wife. This also shows my anticipation of becoming a father and of returning and starting a new life. My written words were just part of what I was sending home.

On another level, I describe some of the things that were going on around me. From the start, I had in my mind that I wanted to write about what I saw in Vietnam. I wanted to tell everyone about it, when I got home and to have some sort of written record, in case I didn't. I had neither a major theme to follow, nor a well-defined thesis to prove out. I wasn't sure what I was going to write. After returning home, I wondered for a time if it would be any point to pursue it. As far as Vietnam was concerned, I knew the ending long before it happened. Like many returnees, I couldn't understand why this had to be and of wondering what became of the other participants-Vietnamese and American. Like others who came before and went after, it has haunted me. This is my way of looking for that meaning- searching for some answers. Everyone from every side of the issue must resolve this in their own manner. This is mine.

A Contradiction of Terms: A 25th Division Analyst's Tour in Vietnam

Re-reading the letters triggered some mental notes of things classified, then. Discussion of current operations was out. My personal evaluations could have violated those rules. I couldn't mention specific people by name or function, on the premise that all mail could be intercepted by the enemy, whoever they may have been perceived at the time.

I was dismayed when I found what my country had become when I had returned to it, in March of 1971. Like Diogenes' search for an honest man, I found myself looking for someone I could talk to who could remember the circumstances that led to my personal involvement in Vietnam. I couldn't understand why I had to put my life on hold, for individuals executing governmental policy, to involve me in something that they never believed in themselves. The people in the government who sent me offered no real explanation. The opponents of the war expected me to accept what they brainwashed everyone else into believing- that we lost, and our democratic ideals were a sham. What all of us seemed to lose was our trust in each other as Americans. After the fact, I was supposed to believe that my personal involvement was my independent choice; there were times when I really felt alone.

Putting it all together, to understand what happened, and what is still happening to others who were and that are in similar situations is my main reason for writing this.

While in Vietnam, My opinions formed by reports, various newspapers, radio, and news from newly arrived soldiers and included some Baltimore Sun Papers articles that arrived accidentally.

The irony of the situation was that considering the proximity to the events in question, the less I knew. The credibility of a source, far away from the events, as public knowledge and was proportionally decreased by the closeness to the actual events in question, particularly in the case of the Cambodian operations.

Therefore, an analyst, fifteen miles from the Cambodian border, doing my job was considered less of a believable source than a Sun Papers editorialist who probably had never left Maryland, let alone been to Vietnam. Local writers playing to the crowd were considered fonts of knowledge.

On coming back, perhaps we who served in Vietnam set our sights too low. Perhaps we were longing to be able to linger over the simple things we had come to appreciate about this country. Perhaps we had taken for granted that everyone else felt the same way. We appreciated many special things that forgotten by people here never deprived of them for even the shortest time. They were not aware that because of what we had done, they did have to go through what we had gone through. Perhaps they did and were just thankful that it wasn't them. Time didn't stand still for us, however, and it was as if we were coming back to what had changed too fast for us to comprehend.

In this setting, I learned to appreciate some of those special things that are trivialized Most of all I've realized, hopefully not too late, that my experience, like those of the people who went before and after me, did count as in all other times of national crisis.

It's a blatant understatement to say that on my return I found that the reactions to the war were negative. I was told that this was 'my war'- not theirs. I deeply resented that attitude, because it wasn't my idea to get involved in the first place; and it could just as well have been one of my detractors, in the same situation. In trying to understand by simple observation, this fleeting attitude of involvement and non-involvement, I've only concluded that various factions and the general public, as a good idea, support wars as long as they can send someone else to fight them. Only when it starts to affect them personally is the immorality of war for any reason realized, and righteous indignation is the current trend to follow as if it were an original idea.

Part of me was faced with getting involved, for my own personal reasons, I felt it was a way of helping the Vietnamese people, and our country. I had no idea that, in doing this, our country would sell all of us all out. I've also observed that some lessons presented are not heeded and quickly forgotten. In other wars, I hope that those who answer the call to defend their country and its ideals won't have to be preoccupied with watching their backs.

In writing this account, I know that there will be differences of opinion and misunderstandings by others of what I did and didn't include in this account. I've accepted that this goes with the territory. For those who accept my contribution, I'd offer my thanks for looking at another account of what well could have been just another ordinary version or explanation of events. If this clashes with what someone else experienced over there- as I expect that it would, or for one who fought the war from here as a demonstrator against it; perhaps this will motivate such individuals to make their own effort to come to terms with these events.

This work is my attempt toward understanding what happened, starting with what was going on around me. It's not a whitepaper; a rationalization for going to war and it's certainly not an apology. This is my personal account of my tour- the way that I experienced it. Whatever reaction comes of this account, I will have done what I set out to do, in presenting this account.

As I present this, I the feel that this may not be enough; because, since my return, we have been involved in at least several wars, and I see the same public reactions on a smaller scale. I will always feel a responsibility to disclaim wars and all other forms of manipulation, in deference to getting along with, helping and loving others, while we are here to do so.

Some parts of this work are introspective and highly personal. On investigation, I didn't like some of the answers; but this is my investigation- not a novel- and coming to terms with it was my reason for doing it in the first place.

Other historical and technical aspects of the tour are touched on to show my perception of events, in the broader context of national and international events. Future projects will include scholarly works on American involvement in Southeast Asia, on various other levels.

My hope is that this work will be a positive contribution toward understanding what happened there, for all of us who lived through that time.

The people who spoke out against the war didn't have the monopoly on love and peace. I do not think that there is a more ardent war protester than a soldier sitting in the dark, far away from home, wondering if he is going to survive the night, to see his family again. I know because I was one of those soldiers. Regardless of the side that any of us took during the war, we were (and still are) all in this together.

The overall experience can't be properly summed up with a few words. In my generational experience, the words that we grew up with and had come to believe taken for the truth can be contorted into things that render the original term vague and contradictory. It takes some growing up to see the world with a wider lens than we came with into the original experience. This doesn't mean that we have to abandon our core values but have to come to the realization that there whole other factors at play that formulate a world view. We also must consider that, if we have any prayer of maturing, these perceptions can be changed with more information balanced with that sense of right and wrong. It's an ongoing process that encompasses many aspects of life. What might sound and seem good and right on the surface should be under constant scrutiny. Issues can be viewed as right or wrong and with being confronted with more information or another point of view, have difficulty in reevaluating a given issue. It takes some maturity to deal with that, which an adolescent might not posess.

On one of many trips to Washington, a number of years ago the Smithsonian Museum of American History presented an elaborate exhibit based on TV's M.A.S.H., entitled "Healing the Wounds". Although the theme was on the Korean War, it was most appropriate for addressing issues relating to the Vietnam War. This is my contribution toward healing the wounds of my war. It's my hope that it will help that process for everyone else involved, in similar circumstances.

PART I- PRE-VIETNAM

HOME

On the green, just in front of Dundalk Shopping Center, is a memorial to veterans- apparently for all time, not specifying any service and it reads:

*In honor of all veterans who served this
Great country, on land, sea and in the
Air, and went forth to face death on native and foreign soil,
So freedom, justice and democracy may prevail. May the
Living be blessed and the departed rest in peace.*

Amen.

Lest we forget

My father would frequent the hobby shop at the far side of the shopping center- the side closest to Dunmanway. He would take me with him. He liked model cars and trains. This was his hobby at that time.

Some of my earliest memories are of Dundalk and the Army fort that was next to it. I remember people who worked there, and the families who lived in Cummins Apartments with us. My father and his boss, Jim List, would often talk to the M.P.'s at the back gate, closest to the rear of the apartments. There were other times when we were in the fort itself. I do not remember some of the places specifically that were in the fort, but I do recall a nursery school and what was probably a drill area for soldiers. I recall, on one occasion, they were doing exercises. I wondered why my friend's father had to do that, while my father had to work. My father had already done that, and he didn't have to do it anymore. It was also at Fort Holabird that I saw a helicopter, for the first time. My father called them "eggbeaters." I also heard about some of the things that went on over there- or at least some of the things that the Army in general, was involved with at the time. Talk was of Atom bombs and of airplanes breaking the sound barrier. There always seemed to be talk of new weapons- probably jargon comparable to other professions, I'd assume. I had a vague idea from watching television and being near the fort that there was a something going on; and this was one of the places that they got ready for it.

On one occasion, my mother walked us over to a nearby airport, Harbor Field, and we had a tour of the terminal. It was exciting to watch the comings and goings of the planes.

These were my perceptions of the Korean War. Why anybody would want to go off and do this I couldn't really understand. It all seemed too serious to me. I didn't want my father to go away and I was glad that he didn't have to, anymore. I felt sorry for the kids that I knew. They would eventually be living somewhere else. I didn't want my friends to move away. We used to play as soldiers, but it seemed that grown-ups took it too seriously. Everything seems so simple when you are four years old.

I had been back to Holabird and Dundalk several times when I was growing up. Some of my first memories are of here. I've always considered this place as home. It was from here, that several times in my life I had to leave it, when it was my turn, to train for and to go to war.

A Contradiction of Terms: A 25th Division Analyst's Tour in Vietnam

Our involvement in Vietnam was a gradual one, and in instances where there were significant escalations, they were smoothed-over by assurances that what we were doing was the right thing and it was fundamental to peace and freedom in the world.

In the mid-Sixties, before these explanations began to wear thin, my worldview as a sixteen-year-old supported a confidence that this whole thing would be over by the time that I was ready for college. My loosely laid plans involved a hitch in the Air Force. In this way, my I could follow my interest in the space program. As for the war, I felt my country was going to straighten this out, and by the time I was eighteen, all I'd just have to be concerned with was getting ready for college, and later the military, in a post-Vietnam era. It was 1966, and this country had never been involved in a war (except for the American Revolution) that lasted more than five years. As I was approaching eighteen, however, we were still involved there.

The war wasn't real to me- not even when one of my classmates died over there. I still had trouble relating someone that I knew with what was going on over there. In 1966, in my high school sophomore year, Clinton Fields was in my homeroom. "Sugar Bear" was a star athlete; I could see him on a professional basketball or football team. He chose to drop out and join the Marines; and that fast... he was gone. In the spring of 1967, while sitting in Mr. Bardsley's homeroom, the public address system announced that he died near the DMZ. It still didn't seem real.

In the summer of that year, I was with my family on our annual camping vacation, at Patapsco State Park, just southwest of Baltimore. We would usually pack up my father's red station wagon with all the necessities of home (as if we never left home) and stay out for about two weeks at a time. I enjoyed these outings, because it afforded us a break from the summer heat, and gave us the opportunity to meet other people, who we won't normally meet- especially girls!

On one outing, we met a group of Vietnamese students who were visiting from Canada. One of them, in particular took a liking to my sister, Sharon, which started an association with my family that lasted for about three years.

Hai Hung Lei was from a wealthy Saigon family. His had a Confucian upbringing, as were most Vietnamese of that class. His upbringing involved very strong family customs that tended to make American family life seem extremely lax and taken for granted. He was highly intelligent and sensitive to political trends, especially when it had to do with his country.

His descriptions of Vietnam were vivid and beautiful and sounded especially meaningful and if it wasn't for the war, it sounded as if it would be an incredibly exotic and wonderful place to visit. In describing the traditional Vietnam, he discussed the concept of Vietnamese royalty, and its relation to South Vietnamese governmental authority, comparing it to the figurehead status of European royal houses.

His upbringing seemed to be almost totally Saigon-oriented. He routinely put less emphasis on other classes of Vietnamese, like the Montagnard tribes, who only rarely associated with other Vietnamese. It seemed that both cultures were territorial and obviously more comfortable in their respective worlds.

As an electrical engineering student at a University in Quebec, he was in a relatively comfortable position to air his political views about American involvement in Vietnam. He would get quite serious and candid in his opinions concerning the troubles of his country and of the absurdity of applying Western solutions to them.

I couldn't completely comprehend some of the things that he was telling me. I could see that some of these exchanges were quite frustrating for both of us. I was, trying to understand- but couldn't. He cited American domestic issues, and government policies, he ventured how we could have time to meddle in affairs of other countries. It seems more valid now, after applying this age-old question to some real-life situations.

His criticisms progressively overstepped the prudent boundaries of a houseguest because they involved how we reacted to each other as a family. Much of what he said was valid, but difficult to apply, pointing out at the same time fundamental similarities and differences between Eastern and Western cultures.

His stays, therefore, became progressively more uncomfortable. His familiarity with us seemed to encourage him to press his guest status, to the limit. Ideological barriers became, as time went on, more formidable.

In my conversations with him, he would express his concern and frustration about his eventual return to his country, and what would happen under the present circumstances. He always maintained that America's involvement in the war was a big mistake, and that no one had asked us to come or wanted us to be there. I couldn't rationalize how we could put half-million men into a place without some formal or plausible reason; I felt that there had to be some rational basis for this. He insisted that it was a mistake on a grand scale. I was thoroughly confused. I still had the unwavering faith that America would straighten this out, and that we could visit each other, in his country, in a much more peaceful setting. He never really shared that optimism.

What I got from him was that his country was in the worst of troubles, and that my country was, part of the problem. Never being fully able to accept this, I kept faith that we, as Americans, would save them. I couldn't understand that some of them didn't want to be saved.

Sharon last saw Hai in Quebec, late in 1968, and ended her relationship with him. After that, he never wrote to us again. I do not know what happened to him. He was free to stay in Canada or to return to Vietnam. He talked at times of being in the South Vietnamese Air Force. Apparently, His father sent him to study in Canada to avoid just that.

When it began to dawn on me that my involvement would be a personal rather that a hypothetical one, I thought about him and his family. I hoped and prayed, for all of them, as well as myself, that the war would be winding down. I never, however, seriously thought of backing off it. Aside from any patriotic considerations, a part of me wanted to prove him wrong, and to show that Americans did care, or at least, this one did.

When I was about to leave for Vietnam, I wanted to have his family's Saigon address, so that, if I were in the area, I could visit with them. With Sharon being newly married, it wasn't realistic to press her for it, and I let the matter drop. It was also another possibility is that he wouldn't have wanted that contacted. I may never know for sure.

SPRING 1969

The prospect of entry into the military and starting life over again in this environment was like living an on-going nightmare of watching a war movie that is going on all around you and not escaping it. I did, however, meet some interesting people, go some places that I won't have gone (voluntarily) and accordingly did some interesting things.

The first concern was leaving home in the first place. I appreciated, much more, my year of relative freedom, between graduation from high school and the beginning of my enlistment. All during that time, however, I had an uneasy feeling that it wouldn't last.

With a "1-A" classification hanging over my head, I didn't enjoy this time on the loose as I might have; but I did, start college. I did use this time by enrolling in a psychology course at the University of Baltimore. I still wish that I had the foresight to expand on these courses, to qualify for a deferment. It's not that I wanted to avoid the military, but I wanted to be an officer in the Air Force, to follow-up my interests in aeronautics and space. To do this would have required, at the very least, several years in college. I didn't have the luxury of time or family support for staying in school.

My job at Montgomery Ward paid meager wages; therefore, I saved very little for these purposes. I had no knowledge of financial assistance or deferments and no encouragement to pursue any of these options. I enjoyed the short time that I spent at the University of Baltimore. Although it was only one class, the atmosphere was a welcome change from the high school environment. My classmates were, for the most part, older men who took night courses directed to supplement their careers in law and business. It was a completely new world, for me, but it wasn't destined to last.

In March of 1969, there was a layoff at Wards, in my department. Because I was obviously one of the junior members, I got a vacation that I really had not counted on. I could have collected unemployment, but my father referred me to the maintenance department of Bon Secours Hospital, where I got a temporary position, for the time that I'd be away from Wards.

It seemed too much of a coincidence that I received a notice to report for a pre-induction physical about the same time. This wasn't the formal draft notice, but it was the next step before actual induction.

I really didn't want to leave for the military so soon. I wanted to wait for a couple years, to get some more schooling. I was devastated. I didn't quite know what to expect. Life, as I had known it wasn't going to be the same again. There was a high probability that I'd be in the military, very soon, one way or the other. Enlistment or the draft were the two major options. Events were happening a little bit too fast for me. This wasn't in my plans.

I needed some time to get my thoughts together, and to spend a little time with myself. I took this opportunity to take my first solo trip to Washington. I had been there before, with my parents, but never by myself. I took this as a great opportunity to see some of the places on the mall that I couldn't explore with my family. They were not walkers or explorers like me.

A Contradiction of Terms: A 25th Division Analyst's Tour in Vietnam

I visited the Capital Building, some of the Smithsonian museums, walked the length of the mall, passing the White House the Washington Monument, the Reflecting Pool and the Lincoln Memorial, at the western end of the Mall.

This excursion to Washington gave me the opportunity to review my heritage as an American, and I was continually fascinated with each reminder of what it was about to live in this country. The experience proved to be a very exciting one. I've always been interested in American history and this excursion strengthened it even more. All those lessons came back at me in new and different ways.

When I visited the Capital, the guide discussed some of the legends of the building. I felt the presence of something very great- something worth carrying on.

In the middle of the Mall, the Washington Monument is easily one of the most imposing monuments to the father of our country, who led the colonists in the fight for independence and later called again from Mount Vernon to be the new country's first president.

To the north of the monument was one of my favorite places- the White House. I've always perceived that the physical appearance of the White House is a result of all of the various personalities, since John Adams, who first occupied the President's official residence, and of the times in which other Presidents, in their turn, led the country. Obviously, some led better than others- while others at the effect of the events of a given time. The office itself, however, was and is one of the focal points, of our national heritage. The newest occupant, Richard Nixon, was still enjoying the honeymoon period of his presidency. Judging from past performances; I could see that it wasn't going to last.

To the south of the Washington Monument, was the monument to Thomas Jefferson. Looking over at the memorial, I was reminded of the young man, who was the charged with writing the *Declaration of Independence*. His gifts of political thought and government service to Virginia, and the new nation, were just a few of the many contributions that he had made during his life. His personal library was the nucleus of the rebuilt Library of Congress, after its destruction by the British, when they burned Washington in 1814. His classification system for this collection was in use until 1890. John F. Kennedy, in welcoming a gathering of distinguished artists invited to the East Room one evening, said that there has not been such a concentration of talent in the White House since Thomas Jefferson dined alone!

At the western end of the Reflecting Pool, was the Lincoln Memorial- a tribute to our greatest president. His administration oversaw one of the greatest tests ever faced by the union. He came on the national scene at a time when the survival of the union was at stake and his life was over almost as soon as the conflict was.

Washington, as is fitting of any national capital, is so incredibly rich in symbols of our country's history, it couldn't help, but to see and to feel for what we are responsible. I was inspired.

Knowing that the military the most likely alternative, I routinely looked for precedents that linked my own family to the service of the country. I knew that my father was in the Transportation Corps, at the end of the Second World War. My Uncle Leroy, my father's brother, had been in the Marine Reserves, and that my mother's Uncle George Tuder, was in the Army in the First World War. My grandmother told me that one of her brothers was an army career officer and held the rank of general. His son was in Army Air Corps, in World War II and died in a plane crash. Both Charles M. Scotts are at Arlington National Cemetery.

A Contradiction of Terms: A 25th Division Analyst's Tour in Vietnam

While I was in Washington, that day, I decided to try to find them. In telling me about her brother, she couldn't remember his exact date of death. I didn't know how much luck I'd have in finding them, but something was urging me on to make the attempt. With this unique circumstance and my curiosity as motivating factors, I started on foot across the Arlington Memorial Bridge.

It was a beautiful spring afternoon, and I was leaving all my worries behind, touring Washington in a way that I had always wanted to do. My intent wasn't really set on one thing, except to get in touch with the world and myself around me. I do not recall ever really doing this before. My high school experience in track and cross-country developed in me a love for running. Running was the closest that I had been to any sort of meditation. On this afternoon, I took the opportunity to let my mind wander, and explore, in a setting that was very new to me.

On the way across the bridge, I met a girl. We just happened to be going the same way and struck up a conversation. She had a British accent, which provided a lively opening topic in itself: ("Hey! You're English!" must have been quite a revelation.) Her name was Sheila Edwards, and she was from Nottingham. With my extensive knowledge of British history, which involved knowing that my mother's family were Tuders, and the bulk of what I knew about the rest of it, I took from Sir Walter Scott's <u>Ivanhoe</u> and a TV series on Robin Hood. I also remembered that we saved them from being beaten by the Germans, in World War II (I know; I saw the movies!) She was amused at this fount of knowledge on British history and culture and was very reserved and patient with me. She was staying with friends in Takoma Park. And was to return home soon to resume her duties as a midwife in Nottingham.

On the way to Arlington, we questioned each other extensively about each other's countries. One of the things that she brought up, on learning my age, was what my situation was concerning the war in Vietnam. Because it was foremost on my mind and one of the reasons that I was there in that place and time, I was relieved and anxious to talk to her or anybody about it. She seemed very interested in my feelings and concerns about it.

Sheila Edwards was at least ten years older, and perhaps she had some memories of how her own country had gotten through a war that came right to them and what they did in that situation to survive. For her part, she didn't presume to think for me, or compare war-time situations, but was firm about my doing what I felt that my country required for this time-, which. I was convinced, even before this, that it was a responsibility, and that I won't have been at peace with myself, if I had somehow succeeded in staying on the sidelines. Men in other generations had similar reservations, and did what they felt they had to do, for their country, and what they felt was necessary for its survival. Now it was to be my turn.

At Arlington, we walked up the hill to the Custis-Lee mansion and checked the cemetery register. I found that there were more than several Charles Scotts, in as many different places in the cemetery. It was obvious that I'd have to pursue this search at some other time. While at the cemetery, we visited the Kennedy graves, and saw the changing of the guard at the Tomb of the Unknowns. One of her intentions wanted to see the Pentagon, and so we went together. We found our way south, through the cemetery, Fort Myer, and eventually to the Pentagon. It was a lot larger than I imagined. We spent the rest of the afternoon wandering the halls. I wasn't concerned about wandering into any restricted areas, as she seemed to be. I was, however, getting progressively concerned about getting out of there and back to Washington- and more familiar ground. One of the most interesting places that we found was a place in which listed every Medal of Honor recipient was listed. It was quite impressive and treated by the inhabitants with a quiet reverence unassociated with the train station atmosphere of the rest of the complex.

We eventually found the terminal, which was located under the Pentagon and took a bus to the Federal Triangle, in downtown Washington. Here, we parted company, promising to write each other.

When she returned to England, she did write, as promised. We exchanged letters until the middle of July, when she had talked about a holiday with her family, in Scotland. I was in way over my head with basic training at Fort Bragg. In probably the last letter, she wrote of how it was hard for her to understand, that, with such a beautiful world out there, why anyone should be training for a war. (It was a fine time to tell me!) I was in complete agreement with her, but for that time, Fort Bragg was then my world. The Army routine left little time to do anything else but try to deal with the situation at hand. In my spare time (There wasn't much of it) I spent writing and thinking about another girl, a pretty, brown-haired woman that I had just met before I left. Her name was Betty.

The combination of these circumstances quietly ended this brief association. I appreciated that afternoon with her. She was just the person that I needed to talk to at the time.

On that day, I cleared my mind of the major apprehensions that I had associated with going into the military. I didn't necessarily want to leave home, but after that, I felt much more able to handle the future. I was convinced that this would be the right course but was also mindful that I'd have to use the limited time available to shop around for a situation that I could tolerate. I was having a rough time with the concept that being in the military meant relinquishing almost total control. This caused me to reason that if I were going to spend the time there, it would be best to be doing something that I liked, and something that I could use as experience when I returned to civilian life.

In choosing the branch of service, I ruled out the Air Force for the same reasons that I had done back in the fall of the previous year- my eyesight apparently wasn't up to Air force specifications and there was almost no immediate prospect of becoming an officer without college. It was to the Air Force recruiter's credit that he was truthful with me. The Marines were never seriously considered- and I later found those instincts to be correct, when I saw them in action at Fort Holabird, later on in the year. I thought about the Navy, because of the Maryland tradition of the Naval Academy, but was unenthusiastic about staying on a boat for months on end. The Coast Guard was yet another option but balked at for some of the same reasons. The Coast Guard was also flooded with applicants who were in the same category as the reserves and the National Guard, who wanted to avoid service in Vietnam.

By the process of elimination, I settled on the Army, probably close to the same time that the Army was about to settle on me. By the time that I had made this decision, my father was ready to suggest an Army recruiter In Catonsville, to talk to about getting in under a specific job category, if I'd enlist before the draft.

I was still interested in law and detective work, which I still naively equated with Perry Mason and Steve McGarrett- some of the popular TV characters of the time. I wanted to get into something that would make my time in the military count, and would be relevant to my studies, when I returned to college.

When I talked to Sergeant "Red" Irving, he made some calls about some of the job-guaranteed enlistments. One of them was an opening for an intelligence analyst (96B), which involved clerical duties in the intelligence field, as well as some investigative work, in combat intelligence.

This sounded good to me, and I was ready to sign up for it. I seemed to meet all of the requirements. (I cannot remember what they were) At one point, the recruiter hesitated, saying that an opening might not be available in time to keep me from the draft. It was getting more obvious that he was trying to place me, as <u>he</u> saw fit. I saw this job opportunity as one of the most compatible options that I could have, in this situation. I told him that this was what I wanted to do, and that if I couldn't have it, then I'd wait to be drafted- I felt that strongly about it.

All of the sudden, there was no problem, and I got the slot, on the delayed entry program. I've often wondered if this wasn't some sort of ploy, choosing the lesser of two evils. I really wanted this, however, so it wasn't a matter of coercion.

My induction was in early June, and reporting for duty by the end of that month, for basic training at Fort Bragg. Although I wasn't really up on the leaving part, but I felt that I got the best deal that was possible at the time. I was on my way into the Army.

FORT BRAGG

Fort Bragg's Basic Training Center was to be my home for two months. All of us were in the same boat in a situation. Aside from the terror of it all, I think that generally I fared pretty well. If we learned anything from this experience, it was that in the military, our survival depended on all of us working together as a team. As we developed a respect for each other, with our various talents and personalities, (some individuals had more than one of each) we developed a camaraderie that got us through some of the most ridiculous things contrived, under the circumstances.

The basic training experience probably wasn't unique to the situation of anyone who ever entered any of the branches of the military service. Individuality was actively discouraged, and the message was that we were all going to suffer through this together- the drill instructors would see to that. We were to forget our past lives and look on it as being born again.

I had been to North Carolina one other time in my life, but it wasn't anything like this. Basic training is designed to be a shock to the senses, and that we would have to adapt to the world created for us here. The effect was as disorienting, intentionally. The most prevalent theory was to get everyone's attention. With this major obstacle cleared, they could put out their program more effectively. It calls to mind one of my high school shop teacher's stories about a farmer's prize-winning mules. For a demonstration; the farmer picked up a big club and proceeded to beat the mules. The farmer stopped long enough to explain to the shocked onlooker that they were the best-but first you have to get their attention. Although physical abuse wasn't an issue, they did have the talents for getting our attention.

Everyone who enters the military must go through this, and my situation wasn't unique to other services or experiences in other generations. All of us got our hair shaved off; they even had the nerve to charge us 50 cents for it! We had to pack up and send home our civilian clothes, (we were told that we wouldn't be needing them) and given our issue of army fatigues with all the other accessories; all of which had a shade of green that got rather tiresome, after a while. We were supposed to believe that it was a green world, and this is what the best-dressed soldier wore to all the necessary occasions.

There were constant reminders of how stupid and inept that we were, and that our guides through this phase of the Army by the best available drill instructors. I was inclined to believe the first part of this for getting into what seemed to be one of the stupidest situations imaginable. As for the availability of qualified guides, I reserved judgment on that. Most of them had this air of sub-humanness, but there were a few were exceptional. In retrospect, the overall situation was probably a sustained Mutt & Jeff routine, which is a favorite for interrogators. The routine is that one of the assailants deals with an individual harshly, and then someone else appears with a shade more recognizable human qualities, which the subject equates as the lesser of two or more evils. First Sergeant Roberts, was the company field first, and seemed to enjoy making us suffer. There was, also, a large Black drill sergeant, resembling Smokey the Bear who comes to mind. Sergeant Evans, however, was our primary drill instructor. He watched out for us, and I cannot think of a bad thing to say about him. He served with the 101st Airborne and his stories and overall attitude were inspirational.

My assignment was to the First Company of the First battalion of the First Basic Training Brigade- called B-1-1. I was in the Third platoon, and it was a good group, once we had gotten to know one another.

The platoon had an interesting mix of personalities. We got along well together, with very few altercations. The basis for this camaraderie was that we were all suffering through this together and subjected to the same stresses. Obviously, we didn't always react the same way to those stresses, for we all had our strengths and weaknesses, as well as our likes and dislikes. Once we survived the initial ordeals of our new life in this green world, and stopped lamenting about how life was before this, we pulled together quite well and helped each other out. It was an improved situation, once the transition from a 'me against the world' mentality, to one in which we were together against any outside forces. Although there were disagreements, when it was time, we always came through.

The personalities were a cross-section of America. C. J. McAllister was from Kansas. He spent a lot of time trying to convince me that Kansas wasn't entirely flat. He was also probably the only practicing Hindu in the State of Kansas. I still think that he was putting us on.

Lorenzo Little, From Rocky Mountain, North Carolina, ran track in high school, and we ran everyone else into the ground when it came to that part of physical training. Lo also had a running gag in which he would announce the day and that it was his birthday.

A Contradiction of Terms: A 25th Division Analyst's Tour in Vietnam

Petrecho was from Iowa, who played football in high school and probably college. He was all football and looked as if he was born to be a tackle. He was short, as far as football players went, only about 5'9" or 10", but he must have weighed a solid 280 pounds, and was without a neck. He made friends easily. It was good to have him on your side. He was an easy-going character, but his appearance was an appeal to force.

Gonzales, a Puerto Rican from the Bronx, was another rough character, who had this habit of picking people up and throwing them down. That was just his way of being friendly. He had his ways, but he was all right.

Julio Melendez, another Puerto Rican, carried on a running gag in which we would do a Cisco Kid routine. I talked to him a lot about home, and he told me that I should marry Betty as soon as I returned home! I always thought that was great advice. (Thanks, Poncho!)

Newhart was an Ensign Pulver-type of character who was obsessed with the difficulties of his relationship with his girlfriend. We met her when she came to visit him, in August; she was a very nice girl, much more than he deserved. He was civil with her, while we were there, and he mellowed out after that.

Manago was a shifty-looking character, not physically large, but one of the cleverest fighters of the whole group. At least part of his success was due to his not looking formidable. He was another good one to have on your side.

Krocynski was a fellow Baltimorean. He was prone to practical jokes, and on more than one occasion got himself into trouble for his pranks. Once realized, the tables were usually turned on him. He learned to take it well, for the alternative would have been physical harm. People like Petrecho didn't appreciate his sense of humor, and gladly let him know about it.

Ned Oler liked to do Elvis impressions with a deep bass voice. We would do Elvis songs from time to time, just to get a reaction from C.J. McAlister, who hated it, but would take it in stride. It was all a lot of fun.

Parker was a stocky character, who always looked like a he was suffering from nervous exhaustion. I think what set him off was that he spent too much time trying to make sense out of basic training. He tried to differentiate between what was necessary to do, and when they were putting us on. All of us could have sailed over the edge if we worried about that.

The classic example was when we went through the night infiltration course. We first went through the course during the day to see what it was like, and what we were supposed to do at different times, to navigate the exercise. This operation involved going through barbed wire, over sand and around timed charges, while they were firing live ammunition from the M60 machine guns- almost too easy. Even through the common-sense message was clear that we should stay down while the firing was going on it was mentioned anyway. I was inclined to take their word for it that the bullets were real. Parker didn't believe it, though, and announced that he was going to walk through the course and get finished first. I wasn't near him that night, but when I saw him the next day, He was almost catatonic. When he finally did speak, he told me that he started to do what he said he was going to do, but when he felt those bullets whizzing past his ears, he hit the ground, and never raised his chin out of the sand through the whole course. He was probably one of the last ones finished. He settled down after that and got to be quite normal, considering the company.

Among other parts of Fort Bragg pointed out, during the outside classes, were the Special Forces and Airborne areas, as well as some of the places where John Wayne and David Jansen had filmed *the Green Berets*. We routinely saw 82nd airborne exercises. Parachutes of many different types, including Rogallo wing, were a common sight at Fort Bragg. We were encouraged to sign up for that or the Special Forces. I declined both offers

In the last week of August, we graduated from basic. I got my assignment to Fort Holabird and was on a bus back to Baltimore, for Labor Day holiday.

FORT HOLABIRD

I arrived at Fort Holabird in Late August 1969. It was nice to get back into civilization, after an isolation of two months. I had seen Fort Holabird, also in a way that I had never seen it before. I was now in an Army environment, but I was also very close to home-, which seemed to get in the way at times. I'd have the privilege (if not the right, anymore) to live at home, off post. This conflicted with other elements of the established order.

The analyst and advanced analyst classes, like any other Army unit, brought together many diverse individuals of varied temperaments. That combined with my own situation provided for some fascinating episodes. This time between late August 1969 and mid-April of 1970 was very significant in my overall perceptions of Vietnam. I was, in effect, between two worlds. One was the intelligence school combined with all the incidentals of life in the Army. The other dimension was the life that I was to leave behind- the one with my home, my family and my private life. This conflict exacerbated by the physical proximity to these worlds. The expectation of a Vietnam tour were constants of my universe. Even my engagement and marriage in December of that year was subject to this uncertainty of when I'd have to leave. Although it was a very happy time for me, thoughts of the time that I'd have to leave were always on the horizon.

On August 29, I returned to Fort Holabird. It was a typical warm, humid summer evening, in Baltimore. After the initial

A Contradiction of Terms: A 25th Division Analyst's Tour in Vietnam

processing, we got three-day passes, and were to return, on Tuesday morning, to start our classes. Compared to basic training, which we had just survived, the placed seemed relaxed. The major activity involved signing in and getting our passes for the Labor Day weekend.

The processing area was set up outside of building 110- a long red building, which contained the administrative sections, the barracks and the mess hall. Because of my analyst class assignment, I had to sign in, also, at a different area, located deep within the recesses of the fort. Known later as Company F, or "F Troop", after the TV show. This would be the company area for the advanced analyst class. After this processing, I found a phone, and my way out through the main gate, to meet Betty and my family. The music playing on my transistor radio was a new song, by the Beatles, entitled <u>Give Peace a chance</u>. It seemed to fit. Another tune that seemed to stick was Credence Clearwater Revival's current hit <u>Green River</u>, which seemed appropriate to nearby Colgate Creek.

My reunion with Betty and my family was wonderful. I teased me about my hair- or rather, my lack of it- and my uniform. It was great to be free, for a while. I slept late- probably until seven. It felt strange to be home, and not being around all that Army green. My father, recalling WWII, asked if I had to wear my uniform all the time. I felt that I had earned the right, to forget it for a few days. I did make a special point to wear it to church, at St. Benedict's, on Sunday. It was nice to be back despite my intense dislike for anything related to that place, due to my experiences in grade school there; but I never missed mass for any reason except sickness.

I heard, beforehand, that one of my classmates at both at Saint Benedict's and in high school, at Mervo, Victor "Butch" Sciukas (pronounced shook is) had joined the Marines. I did see him on at least one occasion, while I was home.

One of my neighbors, Ray Hedrick, was already on his way to Fort Sam Houston, for his advanced individual training, as a medic. I visited him once in his company area at Fort Bragg. (His group seemed even stranger than mine did.) He finished there, went to Fort Sam Houston and in a few months, was on his way to Vietnam and assigned to a medevac unit.

All the tough people from grade school, and in the neighborhood, had developed complications related to either sports injuries or their individual criminal records. Some even went over to the other side, and joined with the flower children, and various peace groups. It was rather amusing to see these conversions, for myself. I knew them when they were hard at preparing for lives of crime. It was a situation turned upside-down. With a group of individuals, seemingly dedicated to lives of hate and violence, a war would seem to be an ideal situation. They would be at home in that element, yet they seemed to be unavailable for service. I could have done without a war; but I am the one who was in the Army. It still boggles my mind. For me, I felt that I could have done without this, but was unable, by circumstances and in good conscience, to follow their paths. I never really understood the term "paradox" before, but I was starting to live it now. Life was full of them and I was just beginning to experience the effects.

At church, not surprisingly, I hardly met anyone else there that I knew, which again, was no great loss. Adolescence there was the pits and whenever I had a choice, I spent as much time as I could, away from them, during high school, and after. I'd more likely attend church across town at St. Andrew's or St. Wenceslas, in East Baltimore. Besides, I had a girlfriend over there- so they were unnecessary.

My whole perception of life had changed, even before I entered the Army. I met Betty, who I got along with very well. We went out a lot, and when I went to Fort Bragg, we wrote to each other, quite often. I felt much closer to her, than any other girl that I had known; and the time away from her only served to strengthen that feeling. It was great to be back with her, and I hoped we could pick up where we left off. My feelings were very strong for her. Following what I felt to be some very good advice, one of the first things that I did, when I returned, was to find out how she felt about marriage. It was wonderful that she liked the idea too. This relationship dominated my whole time at Fort Holabird, and fortunately, to this day.

In retrospect, I think that it distracted me from the conventional Army routine that was going on around me, as well as concentrating on some of the classes. The relationship was exciting, and in the process, I blocked out a lot of the rhetoric associated with life in the military at the time. I guess that I could have paid more attention to Army life, but my heart was with this girl. When the people around me, though, were bragging about their nightlife escapades, I was unconcerned. I let them go their own ways, and left them to their own opinions, I had a tendency, under the circumstances, to shut them out. She was my best friend. The time that I spent with her was very special. It still is.

The most critical on-going conflict that I had at Holabird was in maintaining my privilege of living off post. Because my home was here, there seemed to be little point in the Army's opposing it. The long hours, however, some of them contrived, made life unnecessarily stressful.

After basic, I wasn't too sure of what my rights were, short of learning the difference between the various types of courts martial. There were some non-commissioned officers, who wanted to make this stay at Fort Holabird a continuance of basic training. They saw it as their duty to make life miserable for everyone else under them.

Morale in this class was very low, especially in the opening weeks at Holabird. With not much said; when an individual such as me was singled out, it was a personal problem; but the collective damage to the unit was only realized as it affected others who took it even more personally. Only then, action as a unit deemed necessary.

I first took this attention as a test of my ability to hold together, and to deal with adverse conditions, in the end. Although it was physically taxing, I did win out. One of the things that I had to work out was the capacity to coordinate my time between the fort and home. I spent little time was at home. The political situation in this group was complicated, mainly by going through the analyst classes with a small, but obnoxious contingent of Marines. Before I met them, I always thought that all Marines were like John Glenn and Gomer Pyle's Sergeant Carter. I was even proud that Butch had chosen the marines, and that it might be nice to return to St. Benedict's with him, to visit when this was all over. At Holabird, however, these perceptions quickly soured. Before this, inter-service rivalry was watching the Army-Navy game. Even then, being a Marylander, I was more inclined to back Navy than Army. In tuning in, to what was then the real world, I found that I had about twelve reasons for changing my mind.

The senior Army NCO contingent was technically in charge of the class of about fifty enlisted men, ranging in rank from E1 to E8. First Sergeant Brown, however, apparently had the option for noninvolvement, if he chose, and the leadership of the class defaulted to the Marine NCOs. For what seemed like forever, the Marines conducted an extended harassment campaign against the lower-ranking Army personnel.

During the ordeal, I desperately tried to see a positive side to this predicament. I would usually fail. My father would tell me that it was character- building. That spooked me even more, judging from the characters that they had already built. The Marines that we were plagued with seemed to be without any redeeming qualities whatsoever and their seniors seemed to encourage it.

Sergeant Gabriel was the senior member of this Marine faction. He was, at first, one of the main conductors of this harassment. Only in rare instances did he actively participate in it. He usually held himself above the dirty work, and let his underlings have fun. The whole show was really a long campaign to show that, Marines were better than Army or anyone else. They didn't do it very well, because all they seemed to be good at was vulgarity and pompousness. Their vocabulary suggested numerous perversions, which, if taken literally would lead one to believe that these individuals had problems getting dates with human females, or at least ones with standards. They also seemed to have an unhealthy affection for farm animals, especially sheep, goats and mules.

I must admit, that at the tender age of nineteen, my experience wasn't all that extensive, but I did know how much fun girls were, and why anyone would choose differently was beyond my comprehension. We agreed to disagree.

Leaving that aspect of their collective behaviors where it belonged, (in the gutter) I attempted to relate to them as military men. In basic training, especially when things were going bad, solutions appeared when we faced our individual problems and solved them. Even though we disagreed and sometimes even fought, we pulled together through the cycle and functioned as a team. I also held on to the idea that we were all fighting for the same country. They would, however, have none of that, and in short- order, I knew that this approach wasn't going to work. What I did learn from it's that nobody fights harder than a Marine- to convince everyone else that he is the best. The phrase: "Just ask a Marine" quickly became tiresome and we only used it in passive derision.

I've always held the highest respect for all members of the armed forces and for all the sacrifices they had made; and as much as I'd rather have been anywhere else than the armed forces, I felt honored to be able to be included with them. An identity crisis ensued, therefore, when I tried to relate this group with the people who came before us. This group was obnoxious, rude and vulgar- and those were their good points. Once you knew them, though, they were almost human.

In addition to several cross-cultural differences, other problems surfaced in addressing Marine NCOs, as 'sir'. I wouldn't do that, citing Army protocol, in addition to my almost total dislike for them. After several heated exchanges, Gabriel tactfully backed off. He did however make sure that I had educated myself in all other aspects of military protocol and tested me constantly, to make sure that I was paying attention. (I particularly recall how many regiments were in a battalion!)

This group would harass us with drills ceremonies and mock inspections. On one such inspection, I accompanied Sergeant Gabriel down the line and had to tell one of the Marines that he needed a shave. I rather enjoyed that. It was his way of putting me on the spot. By default, I was one of the more out-spoken individuals, because he was consistently and intentionally omitting references to off-post personnel, or making any concessions, at all, if it even remotely concerned me.

Consequently, when there was a GI party (a detail for cleaning an area) in the dormitory I'd question the validity of my having to be there, on the grounds that I didn't sleep there. This obviously infuriated him, and he would make noises to the effect that he would do his best to change that. He and his immediate subordinates in the Marine contingent, on one occasion told me, that

A Contradiction of Terms: A 25th Division Analyst's Tour in Vietnam

I had to be on the post at reveille, at about 5:30, in the morning. This meant that I'd have to get up at about 4:00 A.M. What further complicated matters was that my mother saw it as her duty to wake me an hour before I was supposed to get up- about 3:00 in the morning. My mother would usually get up for work in this manner, and she felt that it worked for everyone else. Under the circumstances, I usually didn't get home before 7:00 P.M. or to bed before 10:00 P.M.

For a few mornings, I had to deal with this. Getting a bus was out of the question, because they just started running about 4:00 A.M. Consequently, I had to take a cab. On the way in, I met people on McHenry Street who had been drinking all night, sitting on their steps. This wasn't working out.

This didn't need to happen more than once or twice- probably the equivalent of three days without sleep- to convince me that something had to be done. In consulting Sergeant Brown, He told me that I'd have to deal with Sergeant Gabriel, directly. It wasn't the suggestion that I wanted to hear, but it was the only one that he offered. I was thinking of an alternative that had to do with making use of the Uniform Code of Military Justice. Violent or illegal alternatives were ruled out- I didn't want to become one of them. I didn't see myself as having a problem in disciplining myself to the Army, but the Marines set themselves off as a separate entity- which is what they meant to do in the first place. I was ruffled enough to challenge them with or without assistance. I really felt that I was going it alone. I did resolve; however, to give Sergeant Brown's suggestion a chance, and face Gabriel man-to-man, or man-to- whatever he was. I was surprised to find him quite understanding, when I told him what was on my mind. He told me his side of it, and I understood more about where he was coming from. (I didn't agree, but...) He acknowledged my tenacity, and that these things were challenges that would prove my ability to deal with real situations. (I heard that somewhere, before.) He also intimated that the other members of the contingent and their personalities had to similarly, as I dealt with him.

After this, my encounters with him lessened in intensity, and he seemed to mellow after that. He did turn out to be quite human.

Gabriel's subordinate, Sergeant Thomas, had an idea that he was going to torture us with physical training. My level of fitness was high, even before I left for basic training, at the end of June. I had been running and exercising on my own, so these drills were no problem to me. When he had us run, there was no way he could stay with me. I later saw him running in the evenings, as I was on my way home. Thomas did have a lot more weight than he needed, and it was good to see him work out. It set a good example. I don't think that he wanted to explain to Gabriel, how he was run into the ground by an Army "puke." On his realizing this, he stopped singling me out when it came to these physical training sessions.

The lower ranking marines got into progressively more trouble with the rest of the Army personnel. Classmates, who beforehand, were just happy that they weren't bothered, were starting to get really upset, and to eventually understand the cumulative effect this contingent had on the whole unit. One problem was that a lot of these class members were not regular Army but destined for National Guard and reserve units. Most were interested in just doing their six months and spending the rest of their active status at home or in school. Once it was plain to them that such unchecked harassment by the Marines could make the stay here interminable and provoke some irrational behavior on the Army side that may involve the use of MPs; the solution was- the one that I arrived at, earlier- confrontation. If the marines didn't do anything else positive, they, possibly inadvertently caused everyone else to unite against them. After several mass-confrontations, they were, in intelligence school jargon, effectively neutralized.

The classes themselves were interesting, and not markedly different from some of the basic training lectures, at Fort Bragg. The only difference was the classroom setting, itself. The content of the courses mainly involved familiarization with the theory of combat intelligence collection and dissemination, and the various forms that we would probably be using in our work setting. Classes were in different buildings throughout Holabird.

The only snags in the classroom lectures were (of course) the Marines. They went to great lengths to project the image that they were just killing time until their next Vietnam tour. On one occasion, Sergeant Gabriel felt that I wasn't participating in the classroom discussions, the way that he felt I should have. I saw no problem with that, and I readily complied. The next class was an introduction to computers. A young lieutenant gave it, probably just out of Officers' Candidate School. Although he looked like a perfect target of opportunity for the marines; he was extremely well versed in his subject, and I was ready with a lot of observations and questions, I ended up monopolizing the time given to ask questions, and to comment. I noticed, along the way, that this was boring the rest of the class, and they longed for it to be over. I might even have unnecessarily prolonged it. (It was fun!) After the class, Sergeant Gabriel told me that this class had little to do with combat intelligence, and that the officer should not have been encouraged. Apparently, listening to how ridiculous his reasoning sounded, he didn't press his point. After this, he never again made such a request.

Sergeant Gabriel was an interesting character, in a twisted sort of way. Toward the end of the classes, he even smiled sometimes.

I introduced him to my father, at the R course graduation, who pegged him as a typical Marine.

There were several classroom exercises that we participated in that showed how what we had learned and utilized. We had extra map-reading courses, exercises in order of battle- the running of a shop in a combat situation. We learned about other branches of intelligence, noting how they were, by design, not coordinated.

Some of these classes contained classified information and notes taken. To me, it was the most of ludicrous of situations, and I likened it to the "Cone of Silence" on Get Smart. The notes that we made couldn't be physically taken from the room in which the class was conducted. The only value that the notes might have had was to show what we could have possibly absorbed- in which case, just on general principle; it was my turn to leave them guessing, as to what got through, just as they tried to leave me guessing, many times. There was no practical value apparent in the exercise. On my pad, I recall only making about two lines of notes- not even good ones.

One of the classes that did make a great deal of sense involved classification, declassification, dissemination and disposal of classified materials, as well as precautions surrounding the use of such materials. It seemed prudent not to create a paper pile. As a result of this and some other events that have transpired in this field, since my association with the Army intelligence community, I suspected that the misuse of established practices was rooted more in vanity, than in expediting military operations. Diaries and other materials leaked in the past thirty years, especially of high-profile individuals seem to bear this out.

Some of the lectures focused on the penalties for misuse, and the implications that such actions could have on current operations, and of the impact on the intelligence community and the government, in general. It's quite possible that some of the sleeping Marines, fulfilling their nature for pompousness and disregard for rules seemed indicative of the atmosphere that paved the way for certain civilians and other members of the military who had their days in court, in recent years. It's probably more than ironic that some of the individuals convicted in Watergate-related matters, who abused the public trust, actually did some of their time, at Fort Holabird.

The United States Army Intelligence School (USAINTS) conducted classes in all types of combat intelligence and security-related matters, but my experience was in the area of the former. Everything else that I knew about the school itself was from what I read and heard, on the outside. Newspaper stories seemed to be much more dramatic, and James Bond-like, in their descriptions of the place. It was obvious that there were instructional curriculums were classified. That was the nature of the field.

Most classes that I was involved in were for general information and for official use only (FOUO). The nature, history and function of the Intelligence community, with an emphasis on combat intelligence analysis were the main goals of my classes. It might have served others well to have been exposed to some of these basic courses, rather than feed the egos of some of the individuals that eventually have occupied the National Security Council, during the Reagan administration, during the Iran-Contra hearings. (North, Poindexter, McFarland or Casey come to mind.) The elements that tried to portray them as heroes looked even sillier.

The degree of attraction of researching a subject of this nature, in an anti-establishment vein was usually proportional to the resistance on the part of the military to discuss specific items. A significant example of this, during the time that I was there, was the media's discovery, through a disgruntled student, of one of the counterintelligence courses, of the Phoenix program. The press was upset about the ambiguous concept of "neutralization" of individuals, at various levels of the VC infrastructure. The controversy didn't last very long, or it was at least put on the back burner, when it was rationalized that neutralization didn't necessarily mean murder. Because this didn't have anything to do with domestic matters, which was the current trend, interest faded, on the part of the public, in deference to watching what the Berrigan brothers were doing.

An effective safeguard against the unauthorized dissemination of information was to issue it only on a need-to-know basis. It made the most sense, on the premise that one couldn't discuss what one didn't know about. (Of course, as I wrote this, I came to realize that has never stopped some writers and most politicians.) This concept was the official, by-the-book policy; whether it was usually adhered to was, of course, problematic.

In combat intelligence, particularly intelligence analysis, processes information about the enemy at hand. It seemed to be a less-restrictive branch in which to be involved. Constitutional entanglements with FBI, CIA, NSA and the NSC were not usually relevant. We would be out with military units, performing the necessary intelligence functions for that particular unit, in deference to having to watch our backs all the time.

Some of the most interesting classes involved exercises of a made-up army that opposed us. It was designated Aggressor. By not too much of a coincidence, it resembled the Russian armed forces. Their country, Motherland, was a militaristic totalitarian society, bent on world domination. At this point in our handbooks, they were conducting operations in the continental United States, and they were doing quite well. Some fascinating exercises resulted, with the information given. Although, there was a marked contrast between these exercises, and the forces that we would encounter in Vietnam, it did at least point up the function of OB analysis.

My first look at the situation map at the 25th MIC, in Cu Chi, and my comments on recalling the Aggressor exercises were a source of mirth, and I was reminded that, although it made a nice board game, school was over, and that the VC were not about to infiltrate North Carolina just yet. Any old ideas, that had to do with capabilities such as movement factors, were essentially irrelevant.

While never admitting that we were bound for Vietnam, most of the Regular Army members of the R Course had those orders, including me, before the middle of October. It would make sense to know a little about what we were going to be doing. With few exceptions, we were little realistic information of Vietnam was presented.

Some of the lecturers were most colorful; others just went through the motions. It was painfully obvious, at times that some of them were not very well versed in their subject. Two contrasting examples of the types of instructors were Major Richie and Gunny Harker.

Major Ritchie was a short, middle-aged Oriental man, with a very military bearing. His facial expression was usually very serious, but he wasn't above cracking a well-timed joke. He was the highest-ranking teacher that we had for these courses. He was quite intelligent and articulate in discussing his class subjects. His demeanor commanded attention to whatever he was discussing. His lectures were always informative. After class, he was quite approachable, and would always make himself available for questions, and invite intelligent comments. He was a very charismatic individual.

Then there was Gunny Harker. I don't recall his first name. He always 'Gunny', the term used for a Marine gunnery sergeant. He was a holdover from the 'old days' of World War II, and Korea when they had a 'real wars', and he seemed to love what he was doing. He was what we, in the Army would call a 'lifer'. I personally applauded the dedication, but not the fanaticism that this individual portrayed.

There were some internal alarms going off, inside, all through basic training, at Fort Bragg, and at times at Holabird, but they were never so loud, as when I was given information that I wasn't supposed to question, or reason out. Gunny Harker was full of this stuff, as well as the obvious stuff, and it was evident, very early on, between the real world, and Harker's point of view. Oliver North could well have been a product of this mentality.

He was idolized by the Marine contingent's idol; he was laughed at by the rest of us. I did try to listen for something that he put out, that would be relevant to what we were supposed to be learning; but that hardly ever happened. Our scholastic association with him, however, did have its positive aspects. This arrangement gave us the opportunity to observe the mentality that got us into Vietnam in the first place. It had to cause us to think all the harder about solutions. Working from the inside, and at such a low echelon, made it evident that the scope of the situation was very large and complex, and that the answers weren't going to be easy or practicable.

My main confrontation with Gunny Harker was my response to an asked-for assessment of the effectiveness of the bombing of North Vietnam. My evaluation, because no tangible result seemed to be achieved, was that the bombings were not very effective. The old Marine was stunned by my answer and took a while to recover from it. Obviously, this was to give me time to back down- which I didn't. The Marine section of the class was aghast that someone

A Contradiction of Terms: A 25th Division Analyst's Tour in Vietnam

had not agreed with their hero. I thought that it was a fair evaluation, based on the information that was given to us at the time- which wasn't much more than some Time Magazine articles and a conglomeration of President Johnson's speeches- which all seemed to run together.

His recovering comments dealt with our keeping the North Vietnamese off-balance, hindering their re-supply efforts. It took a while to draw the main point out of him, which was the dependence of North Vietnam and the Viet Cong on Russian and Chinese supplies, and their ability to compensate for disruptions in their re-supply network. His contention was that we were, at least counteracting these efforts, move-for-move. We were, therefore, involved in a war of attrition, in a classic sense, pitting our economic and military resources against Communist efforts to aid in what are termed "Wars of Liberation."

Another major point which surfaced was the attitude toward the people that we were supposed to be helping. For the most part, this was hardly addressed. In Harker's estimation the South Vietnamese were stupid, lazy and completely unable to stand up against the North Vietnamese or the Viet Cong, by themselves. We were given to believe that the ARVNs would go along with anything that we suggested, because they weren't together enough, or strong enough to do otherwise. They, we were told, needed our help, and we weren't supposed to question it. This was the attitude that we had to deal with in most of the Harker-type classes.

Looking into the history of Vietnam, even the U. S. Army's version, it can easily be seen that the Vietnamese were quite adept at waging war with anyone, especially amongst themselves. Outside interference just added more kindling to the fire. The conflict between Capitalism and Communism was merely another overlay in the on-going fight of the various Vietnamese and other Indo-Chinese factions to control their respective territories. They didn't need Americans or Russians or Chinese to show them how to fight each other; they had been doing this on their own for centuries.

What our involvement did create, was a dependence on our weapons and economic support, instead of solutions toward the real issues. It was really up to the Vietnamese, all along, to solve it for themselves, which they had almost no inclination to do, as long as we were going to go out there and do for them what they should have been doing themselves.

All our examples of historical precedents and our interpretations weren't going to make much of a difference. It wasn't supposed to matter to us, as military men. It wasn't going to be solved at our level- we were the proverbial pawns. We just had to do our jobs. Personal understanding of our overall military strategy wasn't a necessity in this situation. All we could do was hope, like everyone else, that it would ultimately work out. We were just supposed to do what we were told.

Gunny Harker wasn't the cause of the problem; he just reflected the prevailing governmental attitude. Some instructors would mouth some of these prevailing policies, and, either by inflection, or the wink of an eye, indicate how he felt about a certain aspect of that policy. Harker's almost fanatical belief in the current strategies served to make it seem like he was fighting a different of war than the one that we were being prepared for. It was a serious issue, and it wasn't just editorial opinion, anymore. We were subject to whatever course of action this country would take regarding the War in Vietnam.

One of the main points that were continually re-enforced was that what had been done couldn't be undone. It had to be carried through. We couldn't go back. There were people there who really needed our help. Leaving them would cause them to be worse-off than before.

Given that all of the shooting stopped, with one side or the other prevailing, what would happen to the losers was a foregone conclusion. In addition, the problems were not just those of the United States and Vietnam, but of the other countries, who assisted. Their conducting of their respective foreign policies would be dependent on the results. They, too, would have to live with the consequences.

Judging from past instances, the National Liberation Front (NLF) wasn't very forgiving to any person or organized non-Communist government. In considering the South Vietnamese who opposed them, millions of people would be at risk.

In considering realistic courses of action, the choices ranged from making them self-sufficient, to abandoning them outright, admitting that we made a terrible mistake. (Sorry about your country.) These were major issues to consider- and we were to just not think about these things- just to go along with the program.

Our solutions, to the overall situation, were obviously hypothetical for we could only work with the information given. It was probably another means to smoke us out about how we felt about this- an "attitude check". We had not much more information than someone reading the New York Times or the Washington Post. The only helpful suggestions came from individuals who had actually experienced Vietnam. The problem with the latter is that if it wasn't what the powers that were wanted to hear, they were downplayed and ignored. This was an advanced warning, of sorts, to show what I'd be up against someday, in dealing with the public attitude when I made the first attempts to tell my story. The experiences at Holabird, although not all directly related to Vietnam, did serve to teach basics in organizing and analyzing information, and allowed us, to a limited extent, to think about what was really happening over there. Realistically, events were out of our hands, and the respective governments involved were going to do what they wanted anyway, regardless of what we thought. It grew quite serious, when considering that it may cost one more life in this overall situation, where so many have already died, all this took on different meaning when my hide would be on the line.

HOLABIRD CONTINUED

In October, just before the end of the R Course classes, I was accepted for the advanced analyst class, designated 70-RA-2. I was somewhat relieved that this was going to be an all Army operation, with no marines involved, and I'd at least be home for Christmas. The start of the classes coincided with the start of the cold weather, and the transition of moving on-post for a short time.

The classes would involve combat intelligence, more in depth, with some interesting exercises in order of battle workings and interrogation, which we didn't have time for in the R course. Some of the routine also involved more drill and ceremonies, inspections and leadership courses. The courses were to last until around the end of April or beginning of May. More area studies were given, particularly in Indochina, a grudging admission that this was what we were being trained for, although they still wouldn't readily admit it. The bulk of the class, with few exceptions won that dream vacation to sunny South Vietnam.

On December 27, I married Betty. We lived with my parents. By the middle of February, our first baby was on the way, due about the middle of October. We knew that when we married, that my leaving at some point for Vietnam was almost a certainty, despite the standard lines about withdrawing troops from Vietnam. We went ahead, anyway, rather than waited. My father wanted me to wait, in case I got myself killed, leaving Betty with a baby. I thought about that, but it actually strengthened my resolve to marry her. When I did choose, he didn't object, and happily accepted her as the newest member of the Maguire family. He was even prouder when Linda Ann was born.

My original plan involved getting through the military, college, and being established in a legal career, and then getting married when I was financially prepared. My mother, without difficulty, convinced me that if I waited for all that to happen, I'd <u>never</u> get married. I had found the right girl, and that had changed everything. My grandparents loved her from the start, and my grandfather told me that she was the one, and I'd better grab her while I could.

Around the middle of March, I received my orders for Vietnam. I wasn't going to graduate with the class, and I was to report to Oakland Army Base by April 13. I had a few weeks to put my affairs in order, before I had to leave for California.

I left the classes in late March to get ready for my Vietnam tour. Anytime that it would have happened, I'm not sure that I'd have been completely ready for it. Aside from any fear of going into a war zone, I had become more that a little more attached to home during the time that I was at Holabird. The most difficult part of the tour that I could see was being separated from Betty. One of the saddest moments of my life was leaving her, that Monday morning, to start my trip to Vietnam.

Just before I left, I went up to Bon Secours Hospital to see my father, who was working that day. At one point, he introduced me to a patient who was involved in planning for D Day, who was he cried. I wasn't at all prepared for that on seeing my uniform and knowing where I was going. I also wanted to visit Father Sylvan, who married us a few months before; but he wasn't there. I talked to a chaplain who was standing in for him that day.

I then went to see my grandfather, who lived next door to us. He was rather emotional, though he rarely admitted to such things. Going back home, I talked to my mother alone for a while, and tried to assure her that I wasn't going to do anything ridiculous, like getting myself hurt. It was rough. When it was time, my Uncle Albert drove my mother, Betty and me to the airport. It was a quiet ride; I don't think that any of us really knew what to say. My uncle tried to joke, to break the tension, but it was all to no effect.

Betty was the one I wasn't too sure about. We obviously had a lot of time to talk about this, but when the time came, we seemed to have run out of words. I gave her every assurance that I'd write to her, even if I didn't write to anyone else. I was most anxious about our baby, and that I'd certainly take every opportunity to find out how everything was going. I had all the reasons in the world, and now even one more. I held her one more time, for a long time, and told her that I loved her and that there was no way that I wasn't coming back. I don't know how I gathered the strength to head for the plane; but I did, and the trip began.

OAKLAND

My flight from Friendship Airport was a mix of depression and excitement. This was my first time on an airplane. I had expected it to be much worse, but it wasn't. It was quite a fascinating experience. Along the way to San Francisco, we encountered some turbulence, but it wasn't as bad as I had expected. After that, my anxiety about flying subsided.

The time that I envisioned spending in San Francisco didn't happen. My first order of business, in order to cover myself, was to report to Oakland Army Base. I thought that once I was processed, I'd be able to see at least a bit of San Francisco to at least see Fisherman's Wharf, the cable cars, Lombard Street, and some of the areas that San Francisco was famous for including street scenes depicted in Steve McQueen's movie, <u>Bullitt</u> I was only to see this from the bus. I found, to my disappointment, that once in Oakland Army Depot, I was confined to the base and couldn't leave, for any reason, without being considered absent without official leave (AWOL). I'd have to wait until my return home through here to see the city. I hoped it would be worth the wait.

I was also treated to a little-publicized bit of California hospitality- courtesy of some local war protesters. We had to evacuate the processing buildings because of a bomb threat. It seemed rather ironic that a group that supposedly advocated peace would be threatening my life (even before I left for where the war was).

It seemed a rather twisted way of making a point. Considering the circumstances, I wished that there was better way. It seemed obvious that they didn't have one either. I always imagined California being under the influence of Simon and Garfunkel, Jose Feliciano and the Beach Boys. I was rather crushed to find out that my musical perceptions of California had nothing to do with the real world.

My interest in the space program was overshadowed by my impending tour of Vietnam, but it didn't stop me from watching the launch of Apollo XIII. I generally kept track of it from sporadic newspaper accounts and coverage from TV news reports. Attention was riveted on the explosion in the service module in the Apollo spacecraft and the concern for the astronauts. Through all the troubles and anxiety that I was undergoing, I did my best to keep track of their progress. It reminded me that I wasn't the only one involved in a set of life-threatening events, and for a while it diverted my mind from my own voyage into the unknown. It seemed also, that keeping track of newspaper accounts of this real-life drama served as a critical point of orientation to time.

Our stay in Oakland was mainly a wait, broken only by petty harassment and subsequent assignment to various details, unless anything that had to do with processing superseded them. I was involved in a patrolling detail during the first night and then some policing details during the day. I narrowly missed a KP detail, being picked out for needing a haircut, when something that involved in- processing intervened. I must confess that I hadn't had a haircut in almost three weeks, and apparently this was really putting the brakes on the war-effort. On the way back to my assigned area, I got the haircut.

For the initial part of our confinement in Oakland, we were assigned to a long brick barracks-type building. The first morning, we were up at 6 A.M. looking at the bright California Sun. The time difference obviously involved a regional difference in the time of sunrise, which seemed to be about thirty to forty-five minutes earlier than on the East Coast.

The change in climate was even more of a novelty. Daytime temperatures in Baltimore, at that time of year, might have gotten as high as the low fifties. In This part of California, the temperatures started out in the fifties and got into the seventies.

The odd hours used for processing and tending to various details and basic needs were, to say the least, very disorienting. This may have been aggravated by the bomb threat. I can't recall how long we were assigned to the long brick barracks building and also not sure of how long we were sequestered in the MAC hanger complex before our transfer to Travis. (It could have been that 24 hours mention before) The only time reference that I recall is when is when I saw a newspaper headline of the Apollo XIII accident, and that was shortly before we were sequestered in the hanger.

About twenty-four hours before our departure from Vietnam, we were secluded in a huge hanger-type building; only coming out for meals in the mess hall. Everything else we needed was self-contained in this hanger. We were processed by the Air Force's Military Airlift Command (MAC) and readied for our bus trip to Travis Air Force Base.

During this time, we were fitted with jungle fatigues and directed to send our other uniforms home. We were told that we wouldn't be needed for quite a while.

Our bus trip to Travis was uneventful, punctuated only by signs to San Jose, and Berkley. The wait in the terminal at Travis was probably too short, considering that, if really given a choice, I won't be attending this party at all. I could have preferred going someplace a lot more cheerful. It was rather depressing here. It was bad enough leaving home, but the prospect of leaving the country made it worse. All too soon, we boarded a DC-8 which was marked TIA (Trans-International Airlines); and in a short time, we were watching the California coast disappear.

VIETNAM-BOUND

One-two-three:
What are we fighting for?
Don't ask me, I don't give a damn
Next stop is Vietnam.
Five-six-seven:
Open up the Pearly Gates
There ain't no use to wonder why
We're all going to die!

Vietnam Rag, Country by Joe and the Fish

My original perceptions of distance changed by my first airplane flight but overwhelmed me on my first flight over the ocean. The incredible distance that could be observed at an altitude of eight miles was astonishing to me. The landscape looked like some the stereoscopic views that we had seen in the cartography and imagery interpretation classes at Fort Holabird. The vastness of the Pacific Ocean struck me when we were shortly out of sight of any land, and the only landmarks weren't landmarks at all- but large cloud masses that we flew over, around or through. There were points when even the water wasn't distinguishable from the deep blue sky. It was quite beautiful.

In about five hours, we landed at Honolulu Airport, Hawaii- a place that was, beforehand, only real to me on TV. We weren't allowed out of the airport. The stop was just for refueling. I don't see how we could have gotten very far anyway, dressed the way that we were. (You'd think that there was a war on or something.) The stay in Hawaii was probably less than two hours. During the wait, I found a shop and bought a lei made of plastic and some postcards to send home at my first opportunity. My fascination with the flight and my behavior as a Hawaiian tourist, as much as it was within my limits to do so, seemed to have irritated one of my fellow travelers, even at this early juncture. His tone and his other words however were obviously meant to ridicule me for trying to break the tension in this most serious of situations. This heckler couldn't understand how I could possibly display any light-heartedness in the face of going into a war zone. I had personally resolved by this time that I'd take what comes. At this point in time, riding with the tide was the order of the day. Like every other difficult ordeal in the military, we had to take one step at a time, trusting that we would all make it through if we didn't panic or despair of our lives.

Hawaii was beautiful both from the ground and the air, and I appreciated even the short time that I experienced it. It's on my itinerary of my future travels.

The next leg of our trip was from Hawaii to Guam, We left about 3:00 P.M., Honolulu time. The next four thousand miles was covered in eight hours. The only landmark or reference point was the Marshall Atoll. The whole reef was visible around the island. It was a beautiful sight. All the rest of the trip was clouds and sky and water. Traveling from east to west at five hundred miles per hour was, in effect, chasing the sun. The length of our whole day, up to our landing on Guam at sunset involved twenty-two hours of daylight It was by followed by twenty-three hours of darkness- time in suspension. It was quite disorienting.

We landed on Guam about 8:00 P.M. their time. Our stay involved about eight hours of waiting in the terminal. I think it was due to the landing around of that time of Apollo XIII in that part of the Pacific. I think that if the delay had been foreseen, we might not have had to wait in the terminal. We had already been up for over twenty-two hours and were still around four thousand miles from Vietnam. I didn't get much sleep during the whole flight, and I don't know if anyone else did, either. By the time we reached Guam, I had stopped keeping track of time. I'd never realize it until I counted it up, but we were up for about two full days without much sleep. I ask an officer in the terminal about the landing of the Apollo spacecraft. He had heard that they had landed safely. I was relieved for them. Now it was time to be concerned for me. While waiting in the terminal on Guam, I was reading an issue of <u>Stars and Stripes</u>, the Armed Forces newspaper, with the Guam bylines noting their own local guerrilla war.

We left Guam at about 2: A.M., on whatever day it was. We were now on the way to Clark Air Base, in the Philippines, our last stop before Ben Hoa Air Base in Vietnam. After a two-hour layover, we were airborne over the South China Sea. I never did get to see the Philippines in the daylight; it's my hope that I will someday see this too. On this last leg, if anybody was joking before, they weren't now. The mood changed. It was much quieter now, possibly due to exhaustion, but most probably because reality was setting in. As much as we were trained for, and told what to expect, nothing could have prepared us for the actual experience of being there. This wasn't television, anymore.

PART II- CU CHI

ARRIVAL

The only things that made us aware that we were approaching the Vietnamese Coast were flashes, at first taken as lightning, which punctuated the darkness. It didn't take long to realize, as they became more numerous and intense, this wasn't lightning at all, but explosions of artillery, and they seemed all around us.

As the plane descended, I looked for some sort of landmark, to see where we were going to land. There was nothing to see. The plane's speed was slowed by the drag of the wing flaps. The noise of the engine and the rough air under us made it impossible to determine if we had landed yet. It wasn't until the plane was right over the runway that we could see the hangers, the lights and the sandbags. On this final approach, instructions were given as to our leaving the aircraft- and they were much different than any that have ever been given before. We were told that once outside, we were to move as quickly as possible toward the nearest terminal- to run for that hanger and get behind the sandbags. This was our welcome to Vietnam.

The jet finally landed and taxied toward the terminal. Now that we were all sufficiently scared out of our minds, the doors opened. As the seal of the doors was broken, the cool air in the plane hit the warm air outside and fogged all of the windows, so we couldn't see anything outside, until we got to the door. We were then hustled down the gangway and into the structure, and quickly got behind the sandbags.

A Contradiction of Terms: A 25th Division Analyst's Tour in Vietnam

After everybody got off, we were moved further into the terminal and welcomed officially to Ben Hoa Airbase, Republic of South Vietnam. It was still dark, possibly around 2:00 A.M., Saigon time. The air was very humid; the temperature was around eighty-five degrees, about forty degrees higher than the highest temperature, back in Baltimore, less than a week before. I couldn't help wondering how hot it was around here during the day, if it was this warm at two in the morning. I'd be finding out very soon.

We were briefed, in the terminal, on what to expect for the next few hours. Our immediate destination was the replacement depot- or, "repo depo", about eight miles away. We boarded some buses for the trip. There were Jeeps, mounted with machine guns in front and behind our convoy. I wanted to be home, bad. After reassuring myself that I wasn't alone, that feeling subsided.

Of course, knowing that the Army had nothing but my safety and comfort in mind, I trusted them to come through. It reminded me of my father's joke about a paratrooper, given reassurances of a safe landing, and a Jeep waiting for him. After the chute and the emergency pack failed, he said: "Damn! I'll bet they won't have the Jeep there either!" (I guess you had to be there.)

We got to Long Binh, having long-since abandoned any sense of direction. We arrived at the replacement depot, in about twenty minutes. It was now, probably, around 4: A.M. It was also still pitch dark. Artillery could be heard far off in the distance. We were tired out of our minds, lost, worried and far from home. Now, in the Army's infinite wisdom, it was decided that someone should talk to us. Some general orientations were given, and the rest would follow in a few days.

We were constantly reminded that there were a lot of ways to die in this place, and one way to increase your chances would be to let your guard down. Most of the talks were centered on this theme. Since I decided a long while back that I was going to survive this thing, I listened like I never listened before.

Like anybody in a new situation or new unit, we all underwent periods of gullibility, and it took a while to know whether someone was joking or serious. To be on the safe side, I erred, as many others did, on the serious side.

One of the lectures was a on VD, how to get it and not to get it. After an official lecture on one of the don'ts, he pointed down the road, to the nearest cat- house. (Not that this information was going to do us any good or bad- whatever the case may be.)

One of the first instructions that we were given was to listen for sirens indicating some sort of alert or attack, and to head for cover or hit the ground if something hit. After lunch, on the first day in the replacement depot, we were gathered outside, looking for some shade. It was around one in the afternoon. All of the sudden, there was a siren, and all of us took off in all directions for the nearest cover. It didn't take long to realize that this was a normal, every-day test of the siren. We looked up to find some of the relative old-timers (anyone here longer than two days) sitting on top of the sandbags laughing at us. We were given to believe that this was something that we could pull on the groups coming in after us. It did very little to relieve the tension about what we would really do if something did happen.

During the rest of the time, here, we listened to more talks, changed our money to MPC, the military currency, as a precaution against putting dollars in the Vietnamese black market. As a precaution, it was probably not very effective, but at least not having it our possession kept us out of that sort of trouble. We also received "chit cards", which monitored major purchases in the PXs. I later learned that several abuses that were perpetrated by personnel in high levels, who ran the PXs. I took it as a reminder that we were perceived as individually insignificant in this incredibly complex situation. In order to survive, we would all be living by our wits. Hopes were that we, in that sense, won't be unarmed.

Assignment to the specific unit, after processing was a dominant factor in my overall feelings. The heat was quite a change from the stateside climates of California and Maryland. Luckily, we weren't required to do anything strenuous. Physiologically, this was the beginning of our getting used to this type of weather, and I don't think that anybody that just arrived felt like doing anything anyway. One tends to get too tired to care. You even look forward to getting assigned to a unit, just to get on with the whole thing.

CU CHI BASECAMP

Once the processing was complete, we picked up more of our gear and were readied to go to our assignments. My group boarded buses back to Ben Hoa for assignment to the 25th Infantry Division, at Cu Chi. This time, we didn't have a jet airliner to travel in; instead, we were put aboard a transport, probably a turboprop. It seemed to be a cross between a WWII vintage C-47 and a more contemporary C-141 Starlifter. I say this on the premise that in 1970, C-47's were ancient and had presumably been retired from service, at least from our military. A Starlifter was the most widely- used transport, but this plane was nowhere near as large or as sophisticated as that. This transport was very low to the ground and had a ramp for loading from the rear. There were no partitions in the plane, and with the ramp partially opened, and being strapped back to back in the center of the plane, one could look out of the cockpit window above and looking the other way, look out of the rear of the plane. It was tremendously noisy. This plane wasn't sound- insulated. or pressurized, so this meant that if your ears popped on normal take-offs and landings in a jet plane, there would be no relief from that except by chewing gum. Luckily, I didn't leave home without it.

The interior of the aircraft, (I found out later a C-123) was about seventy feet long, thirty feet wide and about thirty feet high. The back-to-back seat arrangement allowed us to look out the side windows, providing, of course there was something we wanted to see. Being the captive audience that we were, we were at the mercy

A Contradiction of Terms: A 25th Division Analyst's Tour in Vietnam

of the pilot, who seemed to be specialize in reckless maneuvers. When the plane turned, we found ourselves looking up, at the sky, or straight down at the trees. A weak stomach would have been most inconvenient at a time like this. Fortunately, mine wasn't. My ears, however, weren't the same for several days.

After what seemed like hours, but was really only forty-five minutes, we made a landing that was rough. I'm not a pilot or a physicist, but I still feel that this landing defied some basic physical laws- gravity, for one. It must have been all right, though, for the plane and everyone else did get down in one piece- but I'll probably never know how. In landing, the plane lost altitude, coming over what, supposedly, was an airstrip. It hit the ground, came to a dead stop, turned, and took off again, bouncing onto a rough runway. It was quite an exciting ride. Being an old pro, at this point in my flying career, I wasn't scared, but I did walk away, wondering how a transport could make a landing previously thought possible only for helicopters. Later, I was told that, although this was one of the largest base camps in Vietnam, the airstrips aren't necessary. When I looked, I never saw the airstrip- because there wasn't any. The landing may also have been a matter of style, or lack of it. I walked away from, there believing that the most dangerous part of the tour was now behind me- which was getting here. The rest should be a piece of cake. This was Cu Chi base camp, my home for the next seven months.

The next stop was the replacement depot for the 25th Division. From here, assignments to specific units were given. I've avoided, up to this time, reference to specific locations in South Vietnam, not out of forgetfulness or security considerations, to convey the real feeling of how it was, in terms of orientation to a specific area. For probably the first week, I had next to no idea where I was except that I knew that Ben Hoa was eight miles from Saigon, Long Binh was eight miles from Ben Hoa, and possibly twelve miles from Saigon. Further orientation didn't seem to be necessary for us just yet.

Cu Chi is located thirty miles northwest of Saigon, near the Mekong River. It's also located about twelve miles from the Cambodian border, to the west. The village of Cu Chi, itself was very small in relation to this giant base camp. About fifteen miles northwest was Tay Ninh, about eight miles from the Cambodian border.

My stay at the 25th's replacement depot lasted less than two days. There weren't as many people to move as there were back in Long Binh. Our processing, here, was more personalized.

Although the stay was mercifully short; the heat, the plane flight, and just plain fatigue really took its toll. Some good came of it, though, that brought home the feeling that no matter how bad things get, there is always hope. As in other life situations, whenever there is a situation in which you feel that you may have hit bottom, there is always someone or something that can bring you back up again. On the afternoon that I arrived at the replacement depot, I was walking around, looking for shade, and, like in <u>Casablanca</u>: waiting and waiting... A truck arrived on the compound, and some GI's got off, with their equipment. They didn't seem like everyone else, for they looked like they knew what they were doing. Once in a group, they began pulling musical instruments out of their bags. Quietly assembled them, within a few minutes they were serenading us! Before this, I don't recall hearing any kind of music since I arrived here. It was a reminder that we weren't alone, and that we were being thought of.

The unit was the 25th Division Band. Years later, while working at the Maryland Historical Society, I met a veteran of that band- not of the same era. Mr. John Hopkins was with them when they were in Japan, and later in Korea, in the late 40's and early 50's. He gave me a Tropic Lightning emblem- the unit insignia, taken from a drum- about forty years before. He insisted that I keep it and take care of it. I was overwhelmed. It brought back vividly the time that I previously described. Mr. Hopkins was at least equally proud that the unit- his unit had made it through another war, carrying on as it did during the Japanese occupation and Korea.

I met someone, at the depot, a Black soldier, who was on the way home at the same time that I was on my way to my unit. He was from Baltimore, and he lived on Fayette Street, not too far from where my father, sister and brother-in-law worked at Bon Secours hospital. He was, to say the least, very happy to be going home and getting out of the Army. We exchanged addresses and numbers and promised to keep in touch with each other. He also promised to contact my family, telling them that he had seen me here. In my letters, I ask about him from time-to-time. As far as I know, he never did contact them. I suspect that he may have been caught up in his own problems. When I returned, I tried several times to contact him at his address on Fayette Street, by phone. I never got to contact him personally. There was always someone else there and he never returned my calls. I did consider dropping in on him at his address, but he lived in the type of neighborhood that would make some parts of Vietnam seem very safe. He probably felt the same way about my neighborhood. This is another one of the sad legacies of the Vietnam War and of American society in general. In the war-time situation, members of the same unit were treated as the reality of the situation dictated- which was, that everyone's life depended on everyone else. Racial differences were, in my experience, put on the back burner. I'd like to say that they were forgotten entirely, but from what I've heard while there and at home that wouldn't be true. Although I met Derrick Smith only in passing I felt that he was a link to home, and that it would be nice to meet him again to see how he was getting along when I got home. I still hope to do that, someday. This is another of my descriptions which will remain unfinished, until, I will find out what really happened. In looking for someone to dedicate this work to; it may be better to not write about someone who died but to someone who may still be trying to survive the war.

25TH MIC

On the afternoon of the second day, I was given the word that I'd be picked up to go to my assignment- the 25th Military Intelligence Company, which was attached to the 25th Division's headquarters company- 'head'n head', they called it. I got my gear and was ready to go in a very short time.

Sometimes, a smell may trigger a few memory cells. In this case, a minor accident on the way to Vietnam was responsible for one of these memories. Along with my gear, I packed shaving utensils, soap and deodorant. The deodorant that I packed was Mennon's "Tahitian Lime" and it was not packed very well. On the plane, the pressure in the baggage compartment or lack of it apparently caused the contents to come out, and everything was soaked with that smell- which lasted for at least several months. I imagined smelling it all through the tour. That, combined with laterite dust- which seemed to get into everything (even in things that I sent back) were major reminders of my first days in Vietnam, in general and Cu Chi, in particular.

After saying goodbye and good luck to my remaining fellow travelers, I waited outside for my ride. I couldn't help but wonder what this place was going to be like and what would be required of me. My ride arrived in a short time. A jeep pulled up and the driver verified who I was. He introduced himself as Benny Garcia. Benito Garcia was from New Mexico. I don't recall the particulars of the conversation, except to get assurances that this wasn't such a bad place to be, even if it was in a war zone.

The weather was hot and dry, which was something that I was going to have to get used to. We drove past chopper pads and many buildings, which I had no idea what they were for and which units they belonged to. I had long since lost any sense of direction at this point; I wouldn't have been able to find my way to a latrine, and that was going to be important! After about a five-minute drive, we arrived in the company area of the 25th MIC.

We pulled into the parking area of the headquarters company, which was on the right. The 25th MIC bordered about half of the parking lot. We went straight to the orderly room. It was a small, screened building, with wooden planks for walkways around two sides of it. These planks were all over the company area. I didn't know why. The area around the orderly room was kept very neat, and some large plants were scattered around it. (Actually, they were all over the compound.) The roof of the structure was made of corrugated tin and it was surrounded by a three-foot high wall of sandbags all around, except for the entrance.

As we entered, I was greeted by Jim Macrail, the company clerk, and then by Major Fitzgerald, the commanding officer of the 25th Military Intelligence Company. He welcomed me to the unit and talked about some of the initial processing that I'd be undergoing and some of the daily routine. He also let me know that he was glad to have me here (as if I had a choice) and that I was in good hands.

The 25th MIC First Sergeant was named Cook. He was always called "Top"- a typical term for the first sergeant of any unit, but this term was used so often, I can't to this day recall his first name. He was kind of a rugged individual but was more approachable than he let on to be. He was very abrupt and to the point at times, addressing issues directly. He wasn't, however, without a sense of humor.

I was assigned to what was called the 'transient hootch' (It seemed that all the buildings on this compound were hootches- if not in name, they were in structure.) This was to be my quarters for the next several months. Benny gave me a general tour of the company area, indicating important places like the mess hall, the Enlisted Men's club, the volleyball and basketball courts, and the area where movies were shown. I was also introduced to some of the people that I'd be working with. Among them were Al Hill, Mike Scaruzzi, Al Runnels, Eddie Green, Roger Barker, and Mr. Gaither, a warrant officer.

In my conversations with them, I found that any immediate concerns, about learning the Vietnamese language, were dissipated. First, I'd have to understand what language these guys were using. It was a jargon taken from American, French and Vietnamese phrases. In some areas, it was called "Gruntnamese". All of these people, for the most part, seemed fairly well-adjusted- they all hated the Army, and poked fun at it when they could; they lived for the day when a "freedom bird" would take them back to the world- "dee dee mal." Any appearance of a commercial jet in the sky was an incredible source of excitement and caused howls of "SHORT."

One of the things that new-comers were continually teased about was having "beaucoup" time- a lot of time before DEROS- the administrative term for ending a tour of duty overseas and the return to the United States- or "the World". (As if this wasn't really a part of it.) Status by the amount of time that you had left in Vietnam was what they saw. If you had "tee tee time"- a little time to go, you were "short", and that was good. On arriving, with just a few days in country, we were laughed at unmercifully. It was learned, in time, not to take it too seriously, because for now, this was home. You learned to take it in stride and laugh with them about this condition which could only be cured by the passage of time. Cries of "SHORT" could always be heard sporadically, accompanied by howls of happiness and loud declarations as to the first things that were going to be done when they got back stateside. I missed home already. I used this as my incentive for pushing on- something to look forward to.

Being "short" was something to aspire to. To someone going home, it was also regarded as a monumental source of pride to pass on their filled-in DEROS chart- a table indicating how much time was left in their tour- for someone to use all over again. In the chart that I inherited, the numbers were arranged in a manner that the last thirty days spelled out SHORT, the "T" being the last blocks filled in. Ultimately, if you "bic" what was said, you understood. This talk was also useful in conversing with Vietnamese. With regional variations, it was a universal language.

OB

On that first day, I was also taken to the OB shop (order of battle) and shown where I'd be working, after jungle training. Until that time, I was to be assigned there sporadically. This would be my permanent assignment. Captain Debolt was in charge of this section. First Sergeant George Michalic was the non-commissioned officer in charge (NCOIC) of the OB shop. Captain Debolt was going home soon. I also met his replacement, Lieutenant- soon to be Captain Weeks. I didn't get to know Captain Debolt very well. Sergeant Michalic had been with the Army for many years. He was a native of Austria, very easy-going; he was a major stabilizing factor in dealing with the various personalities, in the shop, in liaison with other parts of the company, and other units. He was a rare individual. I'm honored to have worked with him.

Shortly after I arrived, the 25th MIC had a cookout in honor of Captain Debolt, who was leaving. I met everyone that I hadn't met before- and then some. Mr. Perry was a warrant officer, attached to Imagery Interpretation and to OB. He was also a <u>Laugh-in</u> fan, particularly where the "Farkle Family" was concerned. Mr. Brown was another warrant officer. He was attached to counterintelligence (CI), and very handy when I'd lock myself out of my locker. Al Shepard was another OB specialist that I worked with. He was from Louisiana. He was a terror in a Jeep.

He also taught me everything that I needed to know for survival on the basketball court! The way some of these guys played, it was as important as jungle training- imagine the embarrassment of being killed in Vietnam by trying to block a guy over a hundred pounds heavier, going to the hoop. I became very adept at mid-court shots!

TRANSIENT HOOTCH

In my quarters, the transient hootch, the inhabitants were another strange mix of personalities. I was situated in the middle of the hootch on right hand side, as one would enter from the orderly room side of the compound. As you would come into the hootch, on the right-hand side in the corner was a guy nicknamed Rusty who worked in Imagery Interpretation and was always playing some sort of Beatles music- some of the ones that I didn't have. He was quiet and always minded his own business to the point of being almost totally withdrawn. He wasn't unfriendly but would speak only when someone else would start the conversation.

In the other corner on the right-hand side (symbolically, in the opposite corner) was Jessie- quite possibly a good reason for Rusty keeping to himself. He was very moody- which was bad for his position- he worked in the mess hall. Circumstantially, whenever he was depressed, the food was even worse than usual.

Jessie apparently had a very depressing home-life and tried to deal with it from here in his own twisted ways as only he could. His wife seemed to create a lot of havoc in his life and one would be tempted to write her and tell her to knock it off. We were in enough trouble over here without having to worry about food poisoning. He would tell all, to whoever would listen, and with that out of the way, he wanted to meddle in everyone else's life too. He was the type of person who would leave one little choice but to tell him where to get off. His music was depressing too. He liked to play <u>Ruby</u> by Kenny Rogers and the First Edition. I've listened to Kenny sing many songs since my return; and I think he's pretty good, but I had a difficult time forgiving him for that one. One of the hazards of this situation is that you tend to hear these songs hundreds of times before the tape or record is worn or damaged, the player goes home or is maimed by someone who can't stand to hear it one more time. (Imagine trying to explain a war wound inflicted for such a reason. That's another aspect casualty lists probably won't reflect.) In Jesse's case, he was doing such a good job of messing himself up, no one muster up compassion to make him stop. He also played, to cheer himself up, <u>Billy and Sue</u> by B.J. Thomas, another song about being killed in battle because the soldier got a "Dear John" letter. (Under the circumstances, a "Dear Jessie Letter" would have served the needs of the many- at home and abroad.)

Putting it mildly, Jessie wasn't someone to come to for spiritual uplifting, and he tried to bring everyone else down to his level. As far as he was concerned, all women were unfaithful, and we were all either going to be wounded or killed here or become alcoholics. Sometimes, we could persuade him to join us in chess and monopoly. Once included, he liked to alter the rules in some bizarre manner. He was generally a personality that one tended to shy away from, if you valued your mental health. After meeting him, one could safely come away with the feeling that they had it all together, and that by avoiding what Jessie didn't, we would all get back safe and sound. (Some of these descriptions, I hope are taken chidingly- It would be just my luck if he or some others that I describe are now noted psychologists or clergymen!)

There was a senior NCO who bunked on the left-hand side of the building. I believe he was attached to Imagery Interpretation. A frequent visitor of his was an ARVN sergeant named Kahn, who was probably, some sort of liaison from 25th ARVN. He was a very pleasant character, and he loved to joke around. He enjoyed the photos sent to me from home. He always told me that Betty looked like a movie star. I agreed with him! I like to think that he got out at the end of the war. I may never know.

Noel Schroeder arrived shortly after I did. He introduced me to classical music. He especially liked Shostakovich. I acquired a liking for Tchaikovsky and Beethoven. His admonitions to feel the music, and the images and sounds that it conjured up were valuable lessons; and I appreciated that.

Larry Odette was attached to CI, as was Noel. He was from Baltimore County. He was also sort of a wise guy, and by nature seemed very snobbish. He spent most of his time being critical of everyone. (Behind their backs, of course) After a very short time, I had little to say to him. It has been my experience that it's reasonable to judge what someone says about you by how they describe others.

The mix of personalities in any unit, I believe will always supply ample material for some interesting exchanges. It was one more reminder that we were all in this together- some accepted it more readily than others did. Everyone dealt with these stresses in their own ways.

JUNGLE TRAINING

When the 25th Infantry Division arrived here in 1967, the commander who planned the move had no idea what his unit was really in for. From his first evaluation, it seemed like an ideal place to put a base camp. Taking into consideration its defensibility, its proximity to the Mekong River and its strategic position for the defense of Saigon and the rest of the III Corps area in general, it seemed like a good idea. It was such an ideal location that the North Vietnamese felt the same way too and had already done what the 25th was contemplating- only it wasn't meant to be seen. They had their own base camp, which was an elaborate system of tunnels and underground bunkers, running the whole gamut of support for major operations against Saigon. In an exaggerated sense, the contemporary American equivalent would probably have been a shopping mall. Under the circumstances, I could imagine the fun that the NVA must have been thinking of having. They were probably reeling from their unbelievably good fortune. They probably didn't get to do half of the things that they were contemplating, because they were too busy laughing at this American commander.

In the beginning of the division's move to Cu Chi, defense of the original perimeter was an obvious consideration- this was integral to survival here. As the first units secured their perimeter, or at least tried, they couldn't understand how and from where they could be drawing so much mortar, small-arms fire and ground attacks of undetermined size. No one reported any penetration of their part of the defense perimeter. It wasn't something to be lied about or to be taken lightly. It was finally found that these attacks were coming from the inside. Camouflaged tunnel entrances were found all over the place and elaborate tunnel systems were uncovered. The complexity of these systems was beyond belief. It took quite a while to clear them out, and to finally make the base camp secure. (A book, <u>The Tunnels of Cu Chi</u>, by Tom Mangold and John Penycate describes the base camp and the surrounding area.)

During Tet of 1969, Cu Chi had taken beating, and the veterans of that had their personal war stories. It was a classic situation of the war at your doorstep, and not having to go out after it.

Cu Chi was one of the largest and most elaborate American base camps in South Vietnam, and after the ground was secure, it was one of the safest, as much as any place could be safe in Vietnam. According to the book that described the tunnel systems of this particular area, around the time that I was there, in 1970, the Viet Cong local forces were tunneling <u>around</u> the seven-mile perimeter of the base camp.

The size of the camp and the measures taken to protect it- and those taken against it- were on incredible scale. This was an area about the size of the island of Guam. The only camp larger than this in III Corps was in Long Binh.

In 1970, Cu Chi Base camp was a far cry from the original setup in 1967, when they arrived from Pleiku, in the Central Highlands, in II Corps. It was a city in itself with theaters, clubs, accommodations for units coming in from the field, (There was a place nicknamed the "Cu Chi Hilton") swimming pools and small restaurants, post offices, banks and paved roads- something that residents of this area could never have imagined. In addition to basic Table of Organization and Equipment (T.O. & E.), what the unit was supposed to have, on paper), Cu Chi provided the general population in that area with a standard of living that could only have been rivaled by Saigon itself. There were at least hundreds of Vietnamese who worked inside of the base camp in a variety of jobs from groundskeepers to bank tellers. I'm not sure of how this was handled in terms of security, but it seemed that there were a lot more of them in here than out there. I know of no major trouble with them, either on or off the compound during the time that I was there. Except for some isolated incidents and alerts at the time close to our departure, it seemed to be a very congenial atmosphere. Everyone seemed to get along well. A lot of Vietnamese were obviously much better off here economically than they ever were before. It seemed ideal to them- by American standards; they seemed to have it made.

The divisional headquarters of the 25th Infantry was landscaped in a manner that made most of the base camp look like the shanty town that it really was. In the course of my duties here, I got to see a lot of the base camp, though I never saw enough of it to feel that I knew my way around the entire facility. It was quite large. It dwarfed, to insignificance, Cu Chi village itself and Ba Cau, which bordered the base camp. Ba Cau had its own claims to notoriety, which will be explained later.

One of the first things that new people in-country experienced is jungle training, a general orientation to Vietnam. This involved about a week of sessions that involved familiarization with weapons, booby traps, tunnels, perimeter defense and other tips for survival. Other sessions involved familiarization with some of the specialized units employed there that were available for specific situations. At Fort Holabird, we were shown the organization of these units and their given functions, tactics employed and basically everything that was on paper. Here we were given information on how were used. The most important thing to me was just how available these units would be, if we really needed them. Demonstrations were fine, but how they worked in real life was what was critical. This course really made you wonder if anything was safe around here.

The jungle training, to which we were initially assigned, was located in a grove of large rubber trees, which were part of an old plantation from the days when the French were here. They had really broad bases and were at least seventy-five feet high. This area was chosen as a training area to depict, as much as possible, what to expect out there. In addition to indicating types of cover, some excellent examples of the use of tunnel systems in this area were shown. It was ideal, because the VC themselves had designed the most interesting parts. The clay-like soil in this area, laterite, made possible the elaborate tunnel systems that were in abundance here. Most of the sessions were conducted in this general vicinity. A firing range was also set up in the area, not far away.

In one of these sessions, in which booby traps were discussed, it was emphasized that most of these traps could be constructed with ordinary parts: Some were obtained from the jungle; some taken from what we threw away as garbage. Tin cans and batteries were some of the main components used by the VC for some of these devices. The complexity of these traps ranged from elaborate trip-wire devices with crude timing mechanisms to exploding Zippo lighters. Timing devices could be set to trigger explosive devices long after their people were out of the area. Sensitive pressure devices could be buried, just out of sight. Trip wires could trigger a variety of traps that employed punji stakes and explosive devices. There could even be traps around traps, including devices protecting tunnel entrances and approaches to trails and areas for the protection of snipers. One of the countermeasures involved the use of dogs trained to sniff out various types of traps. We were cautioned that, although they were much more sensitive than humans for doing these things they could be, sometimes, as moody as some of the people here. ("Getting the ass," as the sergeant put it) It was also mentioned that because of a certain virus, to which the dogs were susceptible, they are destroyed when they are not used anymore- they couldn't be taken back to the States- a real show of gratitude for "man's best friend." This was probably a subliminal lesson for all of us to ponder about how we would fare when our time was up, here.

We were given demonstrations of weapons used by the VC and NVA, as well as by us. We were shown old carbines, possibly of WWI vintage, RPG's (rocket-propelled grenades, courtesy of the Russians), pistols, knives, hand-made devices such as bangalore torpedoes, mortars, rockets and Russian AKs (AK47's were standard Soviet field equipment.) We were also shown 87mm mortars and 122mm rockets, which were used quite a lot by the North Vietnamese and the Viet Cong in this area of operations. The Chinese also contributed to their military stores.

Our equipment was also demonstrated, such as M16's with the latest improvements including a starlight scope, although that part wasn't demonstrated. We also were familiarized with the M79 grenade launcher, the M60 machine gun, grenades, flares, smoke grenades, field equipment, radios and means of camouflage. There was also had a session in which we fired our M16's.

Tactics were discussed as for troop movement on foot, in convoy and in helicopters, termed "air mobile operations," an adaptation of airborne deployment. This was a war in which helicopters were widely used, as opposed to tanks and airborne types of operation. We were also schooled in getting into and out of choppers, which, in short, stressed order and speed.

We were instructed in the use of the various specialty units, such as Tac Air, Medivacs, Imagery Interpretation, helicopter gunships, Puffs, LOHs (pronounced Loches), Forward Air Observation, equipment transport and means of re-supply. We were also given talks on reconnaissance techniques and long-range reconnaissance patrols or LRRPS- pronounced "Lurps".

CAMBODIAN OPERATIONS

Jungle training was completed around the end of April. I then started my regular assignment in the Order of Battle shop. The orientation was most interesting- even more fascinating than the order of battle exercises at Fort Holabird. The shops were located in a fenced area to the rear of the 25th MIC orderly room. Further back was Counterintelligence (CI) and behind that the 25th Division Tactical Operations Center (TOC) and still further back the actual headquarters building of the 25th Infantry Division, itself. The OB shop was in the back of a small, hanger-shaped building, which was shared with II (Imagery Interpretation). A large situation map dominated the left wall of the shop, which were about twenty feet long and about seven feet high. On it were points of contact or verifications of locations of North Vietnamese and Viet Cong units in the 25th Division's area of operations, which was quite extensive. It covered from the Mekong River, in the East, including the "Iron Triangle," and the Boi Loi Woods. In this area, the 25th's area of operations bordered that of the 1st Air Cavalry- the "1st Cav." In this general area, the 1st Brigade was involved, here and probably to the south.

To the north, the 25th's 2nd Brigade was headquartered around Dau Tieng, and covered areas such as the Michelin Rubber Plantation and the Ho Bo Woods. A fair amount of activity came from this general direction, especially in the southern sector of their area of operations. Another Brigade was headquartered in

Tay Ninh, frequently referred to as "Rocket City," because of the 122mm rocket attacks that it frequently sustained. Some of this brigade's artillery units were stationed on a very large mountain called Nui Ba Den- "Black Virgin Mountain." Nui Ba Den was a traditional standoff point for both sides. The 2/24 Signal was on the top of the mountain, and what were probably major portions of an NVA Division, controlling an extensive system of tunnels and bunkers inside the mountain. One side could never budge the other and that situation persisted as long as the 25th Division was in that area. In an odd sort of way, they lived with each other. Although the mountain was an important communications link, the situation was just as much of a symbolic as well as a strategic occupation.

In one article, I found in *Tropic Lightning News* on Nui Ba Den, It mentions that the 25th Division's symbol was cut into the granite in a place on top of the mountain. It would be interesting to know if it still survives or was obliterated by the Vietnamese.

On the situation map (sitmap), standard map symbols were used to indicate contacts and probable areas in which specific units conducted their operations. The function of order of battle is to keep track of the enemy situation, reporting to the intelligence chief, "the G2". Information on composition, disposition, strength, tactics and training of these various units was maintained by the order of battle shop. We also maintained various files on the personalities and miscellaneous information on NVA and VC units in this area and did assessments as to what they were likely to do in the future. It was quite fascinating to see it work. I really felt a part of this. This is what I was trained for. I did feel that I had a lot to learn, but I was a most willing and interested observer.

In the last part of April, enemy activity was considered average for that area. The 5th, 7th, and 9th NVA Divisions were the main forces opposing the 25th Division, in its area of operations. There were also local units of VC who sometimes worked independently and, at other times worked in conjunction with the North Vietnamese. The 5th NVA Division operated mainly to the north of us, and we were involved with them, in operations as far west as the Cambodian border. An Loc was a major area of activity around this time. To the south, and the east, the 7th NVA Division conducted their operations against the 25th division and the 11th Armored Cavalry regiment. Some elements of the 7th were possibly dug in around Nui Ba Den, and their main preoccupation seemed to be shelling Tay Ninh with rockets and mortars. Some of the artillery, just over the Cambodian border, probably elements of the 9th Division, also was involved. The 7th was probably responsible for activity against the 2nd Brigade of the 25th around Dau Tieng. This included the Boi Loi and the "Ho Bo" Woods, The Michelin Rubber plantation, near Ben Cat and the "Iron Triangle," an area cleared by defoliants to take away cover and to destroy tunnel systems in that area. Local VC conducted sporadic mortar attacks, but at this time, there were no major organized operations being conducted by them. The 5th NVA Division was involved in operations to the south of us. The 25th and the 1st Air Cavalry mainly opposed them.

The activity wasn't really of the level expected that time of the year, probably because of the NVA's uncertainty of what the Americans and South Vietnamese were going to do, in light of the recent change in government in Cambodia. As the situation now stood, they weren't as safe in the cross-border sanctuaries as they once were, since Prince Sihanouk's departure for Peking and Lon Nol's takeover. Lon Nol's government was one sympathetic to the South Vietnamese and Americans. NVA units had developed great dependence on the border areas inside Cambodia for staging and re-supply, and part of the Ho Chi Minh Trail, the extensive system of re-supply, went right through Eastern Cambodia.

A Contradiction of Terms: A 25th Division Analyst's Tour in Vietnam

[VC/VNA unit designations in these segments are plugged in from memory. Examination of media accounts and the materials found in the National Archives and relevant secondary sources, will clear up any contradictions or historical inaccuracies, as to order of battle in the area at the time. My assessment is a purely arbitrary one and should essentially serve as an example than as an accurate assessment of the then-current situation.]

Knowing that they were not welcome there, it was only a matter of time before actual operations would be taken against them in this area, to make them even more unwelcome. They were fully aware that this was going to happen; they just didn't know when, and to what extent they would be conducted. These staging areas were massive. They were developed to support NVA main force units with weapons, ammunition, food, and medical supplies. The complex system of trails kept supplies coming at a very high level of efficiency. Special units, called rear service groups kept these areas functioning. Materials were stockpiled for the next major offensive on Saigon, which was thought to be in the not-too distant future. Every indication was that they were well supplied and ready to go, but, with the change in the political winds, the possibility that these plans could be altered was clear to both sides. Cross-border operations, using air strikes and artillery, had already happened. Some of ground actions may have taken place before the main operations, coincidental to chasing NVA units back over the border; but to my knowledge, there were no major operations involving large troop movements on our part before the end of April.

I wrote several papers for college coursework done at the Community College of Baltimore and the University of Baltimore, on the Vietnam War, and have obviously drawn some of this information from memory and secondary sources that I used in these projects.

On April 30th, I came into the OB shop about seven A.M., and I could feel it in the air that something had happened. Unlike other mornings, when I arrived, there was a lot of activity all around. Routine dictated that nothing happened before coffee and the morning briefing, but it was more to it than that. I noticed place names on the briefing notes and the situation map- places like Svay Rieng and Kontom- we were in Cambodia, and we were there in force. The map was being changed before my eyes. The actual morning briefing confirmed it. The President was going to make an announcement in less than an hour. Captain Debolt concluded the briefing with "Gentlemen, we're in Cambodia." Many of the reports simultaneously were coming from above, MACV J2 and of the division's units in the field. We had just gone into another country.

For the next two months, we would learn a lot more about the staging areas over the Cambodian border than had ever been known before. Curiously, there was relatively little contact with NVA main forces. At the outset of the operation, a lot of emphasis was placed on actual enemy contact, but resistance was nowhere what was expected. The tactical units retreated deeper into Cambodia, beyond the limits of our operations, as stated by President Nixon. As a result, they caused Lon Nol's forces a lot of trouble. Left behind in the staging areas were tremendous stores of food, weapons, ammunition, hospital supplies and documents, which described the set-ups of these staging areas. The captured personnel were not so much from fighting units as they were from support groups. Even a post office- of sorts- was found. I acquired some stamps from one of these caches that depicted American demonstrators against the war. I thought that I sent these stamps home to my brother, Pat. On inquiring about them, I found that they never arrived. I found them later- I had kept them so that they wouldn't be confiscated, or "lost" in the mail.

A Contradiction of Terms: A 25th Division Analyst's Tour in Vietnam

The main result of the Cambodian operations is that it set back an anticipated major offensive in this area for possibly as much as two years.

From a strategic point of view, it seemed like a good move, especially if it meant that I was going to get home alive. The limits placed on the operation, in terms of how far they could go in and how long they could stay, probably served in our best interests, in order to concentrate on specific areas that were known staging areas.

The ARVN units were not bound by the President's limitations and conducted operations around and within the border area after the June 30th deadline. The NVA countered with the Cambodian equivalent of the VC- the Khmer Rouge- a rare, but necessary cooperation. They conducted operations against the Lon Nol government and the South Vietnamese. By all accounts, (except the VC/NVA versions) the NVA was on the run, and their plans for a major assault on the Saigon area, were set back dramatically.

At first, I had no idea of the trouble that this was causing back home. I had heard later about the Kent State riots and the shooting of the demonstrators by National Guardsmen. I was unaware of the impact of this event on American public opinion. I learned later what these events had a lot to do with undermining American morale, at home as well as in Vietnam. It was devastating. In other generations, and in other wars, a successful operation involving the capture, or recapture of an objective, was usually cheered, with the soldiers involved was being hailed as heroes. From everything that I had heard or read about it from here, we were being dammed as aggressors, imperialists, baby-killers, and a number of other names that were extracted from the jargon of the anti-war groups and the sub-sub cultures that backed it.

I felt that it was all well and good to end the war; I wished that it could have been ended before they had to send me there- but that wasn't the reality of the situation. We were supposedly sent to end it, and for that we were cast as the villains. I couldn't help thinking that both Nixon and the American public, in general, had sold us out. I blamed them for not ending it. It wasn't my idea to be here- but I was; and I'd do what I had to do to get back alive- and be wary of ever trusting them again. I couldn't, however, do anything about that at the time, except to do my job and pray for peace and our safe return.

For the rest of spring and through the summer, the routine of the shop was basically the same. I was assigned, in addition to regular duties, to research rear service groups, and the various ways that NVA main force and local force VC were supplied. It was a fascinating assignment, in that I could see that the overall situation wasn't as simple as was depicted by the various elements for and against involvement in Vietnam, in general, regardless of whether they were either active or passive in the situation. To those who advocated disengagement, it would have complicated the situation by putting both American and allied units in jeopardy. To those who advocated a more aggressive military posture, at any level, it won't serve to stop the North Vietnamese from doing what they were doing. We would be wasting time, money and lives, including mine.

I was basically just along for the ride, as was everyone else, here. It was rather frustrating to feel unable to affect the outcome of a particular situation, and to have all efforts to solve it reduced to insignificance. That was how I felt. The fact remained that I was here, and not in front of a television set that could be switched off when I felt like it. It was all going on around me and I could only deal with it with what I knew, and what I could learn along the way.

A Contradiction of Terms: A 25th Division Analyst's Tour in Vietnam

I felt it was fine to end the war; I wish that it ended before they had to send me there- bit really wasn't the reality of the situation. We were supposedly sent to end it and for that we were cast as the ones to blame. I can't help that Nixon and the American public , in general, had sold us out.. I blamed them for not ending it.. It wasn't my idea to be here- but I was and I would do what I had to do to get back alive, write about this and be wary of ever trusting them again. I could not do anything about it at that time, pray for peace and have a safe trip home.

I longed for home, but I couldn't see what good I there except could do, to relay what I had learned-, which I found out later, would be ignored. I also reasoned that nothing could be done in the extraordinary instance of my being home. I missed my wife terribly, much more than I could bear, and that was the only thing that I really cared about. To wish that things could be simple again wasn't really a priority anymore. Nothing would be the same again, in any instance. At first, I was angry that this time in the military essentially put my life on hold. I was irritated that we were sent to finish what some long-winded politicians probably started. Like in all other wars, our presence here was a result of probably a series of such maneuvers. My personal resolve to survive this thing, however, was more intense than ever. I wanted to describe how it was and what we should be doing to solve it. I also wanted to look one of those antiwar politicians in the eyes and address their lack of support. [I was given that opportunity some twenty years later, when I had a few words with George McGovern. He related his experience with the Army Air Corps in WWII and that he made numerous trips to Vietnam. He also wanted me to know that he was against the war- not the Americans who were sent there. He was there and he had more reasons than I realized for the position that he took. I understood his point of view and our meeting was quite friendly. I appreciated his candor.]

Life on the base camp wasn't all that difficult to deal with; it was all in one's personal perception of events. To some, it was one long stag party, with occasional side-trips to the steam bath. To a more serious or religious-minded person, it was a test or a mission, and a chance to do some good. To a business-oriented person, there was probably a scam brewing every minute. To a philosopher- and many of them were made here- it seemed to be an excellent setting for addressing important issues, and safe from being able to do anything about them. To a psychologist or psychiatrist, it must have been their idea of heaven. The opportunities for observation were endless. As a career military man, it probably had its moments; some of them could probably have been manufactured if they didn't happen to exist. For me, I chose to write my way out of this. In this manner, I felt, I could combine as many of the aspects of the experience that I could observe. Though I may claim to be apart from some of these categories, I felt this was where I could make a positive contribution. It gave me another purpose, which was a most important factor in getting through this tour.

Everyone's perceptions of the war were unique. In terms of ideological and military assessments, however, it was only part of the picture. It will be obvious at times that my assessments may not necessarily agree with other observers. There were people who were in the field, or claim to have been there, newsmen who may or may not be promoting a certain point of view, or draft resisters for their own justifications- they all have their stories. In the end we all have to live with what we did. It's human nature for various individuals to have different perceptions of the same events. Hopefully, by understanding this, we can start to figure out what _really_ happened.

LIFE ON CU CHI BASECAMP

Although descriptions of wars, especially this war, conjure up images of all sorts of violence, life on Cu Chi was nowhere near as bad as our predecessors or the personnel who were out in the field had it. Except for occasional alerts life here could be regulated or at least adapted to. All things considered; it was quite tolerable.

The work hours in the OB shop were fairly regular and we were rotated to other shifts periodically. Lunch breaks and fairly frequent missions to a place that sold subs and pizzas were usually on the itinerary, as the situation permitted.

As part of the normal duties in the shop, we were all required to take our turn at the broom or to keep our area reasonably straight- everyone pitched in. Despite the normal routine of updating the situation maps and files and helping to prepare briefings we all had to take our turns at various details. Everyone seemed to get along well and it was a fairly pleasant atmosphere, considering the circumstances. Someone always had a joke or a wisecrack to break the tension whenever necessary.

On the inside top of a wooden card file that I inherited was attached a Snoopy cartoon. In this, Snoopy was carrying a placard marked "FTA." Asking what it meant, I was told that it stood for fun, travel and adventure. Someone else told me what it really meant, and feeling that it was appropriate, the cartoon stayed. I wish that I had kept that cartoon. I believe that I passed it on, as a 25th OB shop tradition. I also inherited a figure which depicted someone with their head up their ass. I don't know what happened to that, but it, served as a reminder of our ongoing situation. Another way of lightening things up was to call for an attitude check, and we would go down the line with our own choice of words.

Al Hill was one of the more levelheaded individuals, quiet- but not too quiet. John Runnels would always let you know, in no uncertain terms, how "SHORT" he was. He even had a dance for it. Roger Barker was a totally separate mental case. Joe Sneed was an easy-going character who usually worked the night shift and he had his own routine.

The officers and senior NCO's were usually tolerant, and except for the infrequent occurrences of V.I.P. tours and inspections, rarely insisted on by-the-book discipline. There was an overall atmosphere of mutual respect, and aside from minor personality conflicts from time to time; everybody got along pretty well.

The Armed Forces Radio Network was another novelty here. I've some samples of the programming that, were in most instances, taped by coincidence, rather than for posterity. The public service announcements were of a type that seemed quite appropriate to the situation, but sound outrageous, out of this context. There were reminders to take your malaria pills, to use mosquito netting, to figure out where and how to take an R&R, to plan for the smoothest possible DEROS- (processing out to go home) and using MPC- rather than American dollars. They also stressed rules of courtesy and safety, when interacting with the South Vietnamese.

Most of the daytime programming, at least from the Saigon area was taken up by pop music. Late at night, there was jazz; in the quiet of the morning (on weekends,) there was polka music. One of the more popular daytime features was a skit called "Chicken Man." It was a lot of fun to tune in, and it routinely stopped work in the shop for the few minutes that it was on.

The Headquarters Company also used the Enlisted Men's club. It was a small blue wooden building in which there was beer, soda, canned potato chips, pretzels and pork rinds. It also had a TV for AFVN programming and sports broadcasts. The club also had a ping pong table that was almost always in use. The Vietnamese always liked to join in. They also liked volleyball, which was played on the court in our company area. These two sports were equalizers and frequently the Vietnamese were better at these than most of the physically larger Americans.

The club, itself, had a relaxing atmosphere, the loudest sounds coming from coming from the reactions over an extraordinarily good or bad shot at the ping pong table. The only major house rule involved not wearing a hat in the club. The penalty for the offense was buying a round of drinks for the house, signaled by the clanging of a large bell at the bar. If the place was crowded there was a stampede to the bar. The day that I learned of this rule, I only escaped paying the penalty by ignorance of the rule, and my extreme poverty at the time. It was all in good fun. It was another way that was devised to remind us to retain our sanity by not taking life too seriously.

The quarters of the people usually reflected how long they had been here and how much they made themselves at home. Partitions, furniture, pictures, and stereo systems, which were picked up on R & R, were accumulated as time went by. Some things would pass from person to person as they went home. I inherited a desk and a chair, when I moved into the OB hootch. I used this most of my time at Cu Chi, Xuan Loc and finally at

Camp Frenzel Jones, in Long Binh, when I wrote home. From the PX I bought a desk lamp (I can still smell the heated plastic) and a fan. From home, I had a small clock, which I kept on the desk. This gave me a compact and comfortable area to write. With my lockers and the bed and the mosquito netting (there wasn't much foot room left over) this completed my personal quarters.

Shortly after I arrived, I received a letter from the Mayor of Baltimore, Thomas D'Alsandro, III, (brother of Nancy Pelosi), acknowledging my tour of duty in Vietnam, and his best wishes for my safe return. He mentioned that my father had written to him about me. He also mentioned that he was sending a Baltimore City flag under separate cover, which arrived shortly afterward. I displayed it in my area throughout most of my tour. I very much appreciated the Mayor's gesture, and I've always wanted to thank him personally. The only person who took offense to this was a guy from Alabama, who was bunking in the transient hootch. He sent for a Confederate flag and hung it over <u>his</u> area. (He called me a "Yankee," which (by his tone) was probably an obscenity in his neck of the woods.)

One of the ways to pass the time was by monopoly, checkers, and chess. I didn't take to monopoly very well. This game, in my estimation, was taken too seriously, by people who had guns, and didn't like to lose. Checkers was <u>too</u> calm, in comparison to this, so, I gravitated toward chess. My cousins, Rick Collins and Ray Lind, taught me some of the preliminary moves, when I was about twelve years old. As a teenager, I played chess with Ray, and my brother, Pat, as he got older. This level of chess was an elementary one, and I didn't spend a lot of time at it. Over here, there was less distraction, enough time and a concentration of chess players to make it interesting.

By playing them, I learned to play chess on a much more sophisticated level. At first, in comparison to some of the chess opponents that I faced I felt that I barely knew how to move the pieces. I was beaten rather soundly a lot of times before I felt that I could make a respectable showing. Along the way, I picked up some books on chess, and I watched a lot of games, finally getting a handle (of sorts) on strategy and tactics. I also became aware of certain playing styles of individuals, which also helped me to play better.

Here, scouting reports on local chess players were as valuable as football and baseball scouting reports on major league teams back home. Benny Garcia and Glenn War were my first teachers for this level of chess. Mostly, I learned from Glenn. He probably just got tired of humiliating me and thought it would be more interesting if he taught me how to play. I was persistent, if nothing else, and so I learned some new moves- or at least they were new to me. I also played other people and came back with what I learned.

I remember discovering, through books and watching others play, en passant- the move by which the advancing pawn can capture another pawn trying to escape from its defensive formation. I got it wrong when I tried it the first time, while playing Glenn. It irritated him, but it did show that I wanted to learn. He showed me how it was done correctly. The chess games with him became more and more interesting. In early games, I'd get into what appeared to be an impossible situation. Glenn would then turn the board around, play my side and get out of the predicament. Later, he modified this by turning the board back and continuing his original advantage. As I played more and looked more into the chess books I must have improved somewhat, for he abandoned altogether, turning the board around. I then felt more comfortable with the game, and my play probably showed He was apparently finding that he had to work harder to beat me. When I became more proficient in tactics, such as knight forks, discovered and double attacks, and skewers, I found that I could keep him more and more occupied. The games were stimulating. I even went on to beat Benny Garcia, (although he would probably deny it!) and would routinely beat David Neimyer, another newcomer, so soundly, that he would sometimes refuse to play me later, when we were in Xuan Loc. After this on-the-road-tour, of sorts, I went back to playing Glenn- and I beat him! This battle led to another match, which seemed like the match of the century. I systematically whittled down his pieces, leaving his king, but he caused a stalemate. This was shortly before he went home. David told me that I beat Glenn because he wasn't at his full capacity. It was claimed that he was taking some drugs and that, if he had not, he would have beaten me again. Being as absorbed as I was with the game, I was irritated at the insinuation. David probably had an axe to grind, because I beat him, but for my part I took this rather matter personally. I had never known Glenn to do that but did suspect that something of that sort may have been going on. I really didn't want to believe it. This was partly for my own ego, but mostly, in a larger sense, I was hoping that we would all get through this tour in one piece. I did see Glenn back at Fort Holabird, and he seemed to be fine.

That particular episode biased me even more against alcohol and drugs than I had ever been previously. As a result, my resolve to not get involved in any of that was firmer than ever. After that, coincidentally, I went back and beat David Neimyer even more soundly and intentionally embarrassed him, to a point where he hesitated to play me again for a good while. Looking back, he might have said what he said just to provoke me, but he paid for it.

Toward the middle of October, a divisional chess tournament was organized; I immediately signed up. It was never brought to a formal conclusion, because the division was standing down. I did, however, win both of the rounds that I was involved in.

When we moved to Xuan Loc, I played chess, but not as often as here, because of the shortage of chess players in the area. I read the chess books and practiced for when I did get a chance to play. When I returned home however, there was almost no one to play. My brother, Pat and my brother-in-law, Al Scholz would play, once in a while. I somehow couldn't get Betty to learn it, and subsequently hardly played at all. Later in the seventies, I was elated when computer chess came into vogue, and devastated when my chess program wouldn't work anymore. I still enjoy the game to this day. I still have hopes of teaching my son and daughter, but time will tell if I'm successful. Chess and writing helped me to keep my sanity better than anything else there ever could.

Some of the people that I was associated with there, also showed, by their example, that keeping mentally occupied, holding onto goals, and a belief in God, (not necessarily in that order) would serve most effectively in getting us through this whole thing.

There were others who didn't hold up so well. Some had seen things that they didn't want to see and wanted to block them out. A case in point was Noel Schroeder. He was involved in a LRP, a long-range recon patrol. In this group was a "Kit Carson" scout, who knew the area, and guided the team. Noel returned from this mission thoroughly shaken and only after a while was he able to talk. It turned out that Noel was near the front of the group as they were traveling on a trail. At one point, the ARVN scout stopped Noel and pushed him back. He told him that this part of the trail was booby-trapped, and that he would go ahead of him to check it out. The scout went a little further up the trail and almost immediately stepped on a land mine. It was difficult for Noel to comprehend that the scout wasn't there anymore. He had just been talking to him a minute ago... and then he was gone. Noel concluded by saying that he needed a drink. He wasn't the same for quite a while.

Drinking was one of the ways that people in this situation dealt with their problems. Actually, this was one of the most common means. A lot is made of the drug problem, in regard to servicemen in Vietnam. It was nowhere near as commonplace as the abuse of alcohol. Both were devastating. Although this type of escape seemed justified in cases like this, Noel's circumstances were more the exception, rather than the rule. Any excuse seemed to be used for this. It wasn't, however, a problem that was necessarily acquired here. It was more than likely a problem that they had brought with them. Peer pressure was also a major mitigating circumstance. It was considered a popular way of coping- it's an old story.

The drugs may have come from other countries, not always from Vietnam, and the atmosphere that precipitated their use and misuse was rooted in the sixties culture that glorified drugs and other escapes from reality.

I felt that, especially in this most serious of situations, I'd need all of my faculties in working order if I expected to survive this tour. Using something that would alter those senses in any way could prove either directly or indirectly disastrous. Even though this was a support situation, everyone's life still depended on everyone else's, and, if that were impaired, someone could be injured or killed. It was much more than a personal matter, for what they did affected everyone around them- not only themselves. My life sometimes depended on the alertness of the people that I was working with. Not everyone agreed with this outlook, and I was often chided for my caution. My stand was sometimes interpreted as self-righteousness, or timidity. As in other situations, peer pressure constantly issued challenges to our personal convictions. Some individuals played on fearfulness to disagree with what seemed, at times, to be the popular consensus. Being about two years out of high school, those messages sounded rather similar. Now, I could at least see the necessity for trusting my feelings. It also seemed like a good opportunity to act on them.

Among these challenges, another popular argument went that this was not part of the real world, and that what was done here didn't matter much- after all, who would know? My answer would be that *I'd* know, and I've to live with me. I also felt stronger about being prepared, spiritually. If I were to die here, considering my beliefs in the final judgment, blaming it on someone else won't be a valid defense. I was taught that I'd be held accountable for what I did. I never considered finger pointing as an option.

I was sufficiently scared enough to stay out of most of that trouble. I don't feel, however, that I've to confess my sins here or at any time; but as far as I'm concerned, any short-comings that I might have had, can be chalked up to ignorance, rather than malice or any of the obvious vices at hand.

At any rate, I was still pretty sensitive to criticism and didn't really know how to respond appropriately; consequently, when an expedition was organized to a local bar or a steam bath I stayed behind, sharpening my writing and chess skills. I don't feel that I suffered in the long run, and I don't have any problems with my conscience. All of us had uncertainties as to how we were perceived by each other, and never readily admit how really scared we were, considering the overall situation. It was just manifested in as many different ways as there are people.

I did learn to respect individual choices in religion, morals, and ethics. I didn't necessarily agree with all of them, but I respected them. I also learned not to expect the same understanding in return. In the final analysis, I still hope that I was much stronger for the lessons.

WEATHER

The climate was fairly consistent throughout the year, varying only between very hot and very rainy. The weather was altered significantly only by the summer and autumn monsoons. These rainy periods occurred from the middle of May to the end of June, and then from the middle of September to the end of October.

At the start of these periods, it would start to rain at around 4:00 P.M., and stop at around six-thirty. One could almost set a watch by it. Even if it didn't look like it was going to rain, several minutes before, the clouds would quickly roll in, and the rain start on time. It was also beautiful to watch.

The amount of rain that came down, in just a short period of time was amazing. They were routinely worse than the heaviest downpours that I saw back home in Baltimore. In these downpours, visibility was reduced to almost nothing, and the noise that it made on the tin roofing made verbal communication out of the question. The only thing to do was to watch the rain and wait until it slacked up.

In the transient quarters, where I bunked, during the first rains, I noticed that the concrete base wasn't built up high enough to keep us out of water- most of the time. As a result, on these rainy days, water would come in on the orderly room side. When it was really bad, it would come in both doors, and sometimes the side walls. Photos that were taken of the quarters show examples of this. It was usually quite a lot of water in a brief amount of time, and this would be just about every day, during the monsoon seasons. It was easy to see why this land was particularly suited for growing rice. It got to be quite swamp-like. I quickly found out what those wooden planks were all about- they were necessary to get around. It was also very difficult to keep clothes dry, when it rained all day, at the height of the rainy seasons. These were the only times of the year when it wasn't hot. There were few variations here between hot and wet. After a few days of this, the heat wasn't all that bad. Bunker guard was especially uncomfortable, however, on nights when it rained constantly. .Life in rain gear was a major necessity and one learned rapidly to take extra clothes- preferably dry- to survive this detail. A field jacket seemed just perfect for the occasion, as long as it didn't get too wet. It was also nice to have a good supply of dry socks. It would get pretty cold out there.

The heat was something that we had to adjust to. At first, it was very difficult, coming from an area where the daytime high temperatures were forty degrees lower than the nighttime lows, here. Were warned to always wear appropriate clothing, and a hat for protection from the sun. The sun was so intense; here burns could result from extended exposure, especially if one were not used to it. I learned the hard way. I was burned so badly, when I first got there, that it was a long time before I took my shirt off again during the day. I had a difficult time understanding how I could get burned like that in the beginning of May. A lot of guys on the compound would, in off-duty hours, go around without shirts. I followed suit, and I paid dearly for it. It didn't occur to me at the time that I had to get used to it. The sun really did a job on me. It's funny, in retrospect, but it was most painful, at the time.

I noticed that a lot of these guys, including the Blacks, would intentionally tan, just before they went home. This was referred to as a "DEROS tan." I got mine in March, just before I returned. I felt this was a ritual worth observing.

Once it was understood, what skin could and couldn't take, one would dress accordingly. After hours, we could wear what we wanted, so I wrote home for Betty to send some shorts and sports shirts.

When the sun went down, it was quite comfortable. Sleeping wasn't so bad, when an electric fan could be bought and positioned correctly. Once accustomed to the high temperatures here, the rain seemed to change everything. When it rained constantly, the temperatures would go down into the seventies, making it feel like a cold snap.

RELIGIOUS SERVICES

Religious services were available at Cu Chi base camp on Sundays. The services that I attended were rather informal. The first time that I attended a service in Cu Chi I attended a Methodist service, accidentally. The chaplain explained that there may be times when only a certain chaplain would be available, and in a situation like this, such a mistake could be understood. He also pointed out that the various denominational services were modified just for this situation. None-the-less, I attended the Catholic service, just to cover myself!

The Catholic mass, as celebrated here, was slightly modified. There is a part in the beginning of the mass, in which a conditional absolution is given. In this situation of questionable availability of Catholic priests, in the area, this absolution was given, in case of one being in a questionable state of grace. Communion could be taken, on condition that a good confession is made, at the earliest opportunity. This was mainly for the benefit of soldiers in the field, who were even farther away from regular services. In my first confession, I mentioned the incident about the Methodist services, and the priest concurred with the minister. The chaplain probably spent a large part of the week, in the field, and reserved Sundays for services, at the base camp chapel. Civilian workers on the base camp and Catholic Vietnamese would also be present at these services, in front of main headquarters building, across the road. One of the things that I received from going to that chapel, was a rosary made out of cord, olive drab (Of course!) I received another one later. I still have them in my possession.

DETAILS

As part of this unit, we were all required to make ourselves available for various details, and, as an attached unit of Headquarters Company, we all pulled K.P. and bunker guard at various intervals. Nothing in the OB shop, no matter how important it seemed, took precedence over these details. NCO's were required to do charge of quarters in 25th MIC, and the E4's and below were required to do the other details which included a grounds-keeping detail with the Vietnamese, along with keeping our living quarters in reasonable condition. Inspections were not all that stringent. Company formations were required, but the formality of it was held to a minimum.

Only K.P. seemed to be the most forced-labor type of assignment. It involved being in the mess hall at around five in the morning, and being there until around seven in the evening, when everything was finished. I never really relished the potato-peeling bit, and the continuous cleaning up, that this assignment involved. It wasn't, however, as bad as it could have been, because we worked with some Vietnamese women, and we helped each other out. Because they knew their way around, we usually just followed their lead.

Jessie was one of the NCO's that had to be dealt with here, but he wasn't as terrible as he could have been. His senior was pretty tolerant, and he would usually countermand Jessie, if he tried to mistreat us.

The main Vietnamese worker there was a lady, who was married to an ARVN soldier, and she was about six months pregnant. She was pretty nice to work with, and it made those days pass a lot faster, when she was there. I talked about my wife's baby being due in October; and whenever she saw me, she would always ask about the latest news from home on its progress.

Jessie would always hold out the threat of making us clean out the grease trap, but he never followed through, because the sergeant would always stop him, from carrying out such outrageous details. It was never cleaned, as far as I know. Someday, Vietnamese archeologists will happen upon these fabled landmarks and may sue us for its environmental impact. They'll probably start blaming Americans for such damages all over again.

The K.P. detail came up about every six weeks. I pulled it about three or four times before the division stood down, and we prepared to move to Xuan Loc.

The food was tolerable, but it had a lot of starch. The milk was of a processed type, and it really didn't taste quite like milk. It was probably as good as the Army could do at the time. We got used to it, but it was great to taste real milk again, when I returned. Fruit seemed to be one of the safest bets. Bananas were probably the only fruit that was native to here. The drawback to this was that by the time the bananas got to us they were either green or black- never yellow. If they were green, they were inedible. If they were black, they were also soft and mushy; there seemed to be no in-between. My curiosity was satisfied, eventually, as to what types of large plants were all over the 25th MIC compound, when I saw bananas on them. The good ones were grabbed up, before they reached the mess hall. As for the rest of the food, like adjusting to the weather, it took a while. I was just hoping to survive it. Fortunately, there was the E.M. club and the P.X., where canned and packaged food could be stockpiled, for the time when food in the mess hall was too terrible to deal with. At Cu Chi, we couldn't keep regular food in our quarters, (I can't think of why anyone would want to take anything from the mess hall, anyway, unless they had a death wish) but we could keep canned items and C-rations, as long as we didn't litter our areas. We also would draw C-rations whenever we went on bunker guard. Some of that stuff was quite revolting. Sometimes, only the peanut butter and crackers were edible. It made it even less appetizing, on being told out that we were probably eating food that may have been packed for the Korean War- before many of us were born.

Some of the things that could be heated up weren't so terrible. It was, many times, a reasonable alternative to the mess hall. Usually, the only time that we didn't get meals out of the headquarters company mess hall was when we drew bunker guard, or if we worked evenings in the OB shop. For bunker guard, in addition to drawing rations, we sometimes got sandwiches and coffee. The only drawback to this was that the detail was usually late, and by the time it arrived, the coffee was cold, and the sandwiches were stale. It did, however, serve the purpose of keeping us uncomfortable, and subsequently, awake. Sometimes, mercifully, they didn't come.

Evening duty in the OB shop supplied us with a built-in break time. If we broke fairly early, we could go to a place where the Vietnamese could make a pizza that was full of cheese and riddled with mushrooms. If we broke after about eight-thirty, we could go over to the MPs mess. Before I discovered this place, I thought that all mess halls were as bad as ours. It wasn't true at all; the food there was great. I remember, particularly, biscuits that were fresh out of the oven, and meat and potatoes that tasted like they were supposed to taste- real. It was almost made you think about hanging out with the MPs more often.

BUNKER GUARD

Another company detail that we were involved in was bunker guard. This came up about once a month. This involved spending a night out on the perimeter, in a bunker that was assigned to us, as part of the headquarters company contingent. The rotation of the different units staffing Headquarters Company enabled us to meet many different individuals. I don't think that any two assignments ever yielded the same combination of three people. This detail was, for the most part, quiet. The only variables were who was assigned, and an occasional "mad minute," a designated time to test-fire our weapons, if we chose. This would happen when we would be given the clearance over the field phone. I didn't especially go for that, because it involved cleaning the weapon in the morning. I'd rather have taken the time to shower and sleep. After this detail, I could sleep through the morning, and be ready for afternoon work in the OB shop. We could do that if we could filter out all the daily commotion. When we did get to the office, we only had to work a half of the day.

Bunker guard wasn't a bad assignment, if it didn't rain, in which case it could really get uncomfortably cold. The fall monsoon made it even worse. Sometimes I felt like I was going to freeze to death.

Another hazard was the mosquitoes and other insects that would get really thick, on nights that it didn't rain. There were two main measures taken to survive the mosquitoes. The first is that the repellent that we were given had to be used. It smelled terrible, but there wasn't anyone there to impress, anyway. If the repellent was applied properly, to the exposed areas and clothes openings, it minimized the amount of bites significantly. It had to be applied every few hours, or all the insects in the immediate area would sense that it was mealtime, and you would be the meal. The other precaution taken was the use of mosquito netting over the helmet. When worn in a manner that kept the insects from getting near your face, it worked pretty well. It wasn't exactly what the best-dressed soldier was wearing, but it worked quite well, when necessary.

During bunker guard, there were a few diversions that were available to us. We talked a lot about what we had gone through here and of whatever was going on back home. We could look at the perimeter and philosophize about here and home. We would also get the latest news from home from people who just arrived from the states; some of it wasn't all that pleasant. It often made us wonder if this wasn't the safer here.

In this situation, conversation was quite meaningful. There was little in the way of distraction, except what was troubling us on the inside. The only outside sounds and sights were usually far off, and we hoped was unconnected to what we had to deal with that particular night. Activities ranged from bull sessions, to Tai Quan Do lessons.

The major landmark that could be seen from this vantage point was off to the northeast. Nui Ba Den, "Black Virgin Mountain," was the most prominent of several rises in the flat landscape between Cu Chi and the Cambodian border, about fifteen miles away. An artillery unit and a communications facility were stationed on top of the mountain, along with 2/24th Signal. It was said at that time that a North Vietnamese regiment was dug into the mountain. For the whole time that the Twenty-fifth Division was here, it prompted stories of the legendary standoff that I mentioned previously. From our bunker on the perimeter, we could see the lights that indicated the perimeter of the compound on top of the mountain. I was told that from that mountain, on a clear night, the lights of Saigon could be seen.

As stark and barren as this landscape was, the sky and outline of the mountain were beautiful sights. It was fascinating to be able to see such a long way, watching choppers take off and land from great distances. One time, I watched a Chinook helicopter, usually the type used for transport, carry a net full of supplies under it for a very long distance, to the north or northeast, possibly toward Dau Tieng, where some units of one of our brigades was deployed. The sky was fairly clear, and it had not gotten dark, yet, and I watched it until it was about to land.

As the sun set, the lights on Nui Ba Den would begin to appear, twinkling, at first, then brighter, until the line of lights near the top of the mountain were well defined. As it became darker, the mountain disappeared, and only the lights were visible. If the weather was bad, the mountain would vanish, altogether, being easily lost in the fog, leaving the barbed wire and claymore mines visible just outside of our perimeter. It was spooky, whenever that happened.

In the quiet of the bunker, we looked toward the east, and Cambodia; we hoped that nothing would happen. This time out here afforded us opportunities to think out loud- sometimes, possibly, too loud. We would share our personal views of involvement here. In this setting, it led to some very animated conversations, about why we should or shouldn't be here, and what was going on at home in connection with the war.

A Contradiction of Terms: A 25th Division Analyst's Tour in Vietnam

On one occasion, after I had been on bunker guard several times, one individual assigned to our bunker provided some very interesting insights as to how he felt about how things were going. He had just arrived several weeks before, and wasn't even finished jungle training, but he was out here with us. He was already crazy, and he just got here. His views, although, not fully thought out, and certainly not what I wanted to hear at the time, were, none-the-less, thought provoking. Apparently, he had left the states shortly after the fallout from the events at Kent State, in May. From the way that he described it, the happenings there had a profound impact on a lot of people. He was plainly upset and over our role here and had more sympathy for the individuals who had gone to Canada, than us- but yet he was here with us. His heart was with them, but his body was here, and his brains were nowhere to be found. We were out here on this perimeter because there were people out there who didn't have our safety in mind. I'd rather that he didn't give them any help.

His view was an interesting concept, and I'm not even sure that this profundity, on his part, was intentional; but there was something there that was worth pondering. I felt, however, that the chances of dying violently in Montreal were considerably less than here- so I couldn't easily summon up concerns for the safety of one of his idealist heroes.

It would, I agreed, be a most difficult thing to leave your home and loved ones- who you may never see again, to go to a strange country, to do something that one felt was right. I sort of remembered doing something like that, but that was months ago. I reasoned that either course would probably require equal amounts of courage. How could we know what was the proper course? This had all the earmarks of one of life's more important lessons. Resolutions, including mine, were probably not all that coherent. The answer, I felt, had something to do with having the satisfaction of knowing that what was done was for the good. The catcher to this is that one may not ever have the satisfaction of knowing. It may never be given. We therefore resigned ourselves to that possibility rather readily.

This guy was plainly spooked by the whole thing. Someone or something convinced him that he was doing a cowardly thing by going along with what was perceived as the program. He was also convinced that we were all being lied to. I already knew that, I just stopped getting upset about it. He was disturbed to the extent that he didn't know what to believe, and it had unraveled him. He was psychologically immobilized. I liked, less and less, the idea of trusting this guy with an M60 machine gun, or any other weapon. He was scared, but I was scared for a different reason. He was already beaten. If my survival depended on individuals like that, and I'd just as soon have not had him there, contributing to the confusion. This not being my call, I had to put up with it. I didn't want to be here either, but I had to deal with what was going on there at the time.

On very clear nights, when the moon was full, illumination was such that we could see several hundred feet in front of us. We would also take turns on the "starlight scope," a device with which you could see in the dark. The green tint made everything look like a moonscape. The best use that we made of this was for watching for who was approaching from behind us. Roving patrols, which were responsible for patrolling given sectors, would stop by from time to time. Sometimes, they came by jeep, other times, on foot.

Periodically, we would also get calls, on the field phone, for communications checks (commo checks) and special instructions, which would be given. Sometimes we would initiate commo checks, cranking up the field phone and clipping the receiver back into its holder, after we were finished. It gave us the feeling that we weren't completely alone, out there, and that some of them were even on our side.

Bunker guard was always one of the quieter times, in a tour of duty over here. It was also my personal hope that it would always remain so. With seemingly nothing, but time, on our hands, and hoping that nothing would happen, we did get to talk about a lot of good things too.

When appropriate, we would sleep in shifts. Two or three of us would be on at the same time. One occasion, I was given a few lessons, by Joe Garza, on Tai Quan Do. It was mainly a lesson on pressure points. It was quite interesting and empowering.

The only ones that routinely came by our bunker were the NCOs in charge of the sector, and the detail that came around with the coffee and sandwiches. They would usually show up around three or four in the morning. In reference to the later, by the time this detail got around to us, there was nothing edible, and it was almost breakfast, anyway. I do believe, however, that they meant well, and I did appreciate them being out there for us, at that time of the morning.

DAY WORKERS

The only other major detail was a company detail involving supervision of the Vietnamese day-workers on duties like policing the company area, burning waste and generally cleaning up where necessary. This group was composed of all women, except for one elderly man, named Mui Tan. Mui was the Vietnamese equivalent of Mister. The women were of varying ages, the oldest apparently being the leader. Her name was Ba Hai. She was wrinkled, chewed beetle nut, and her teeth showed it. The Vietnamese word "Ba" was the term to denote a married woman. An unmarried woman was addressed as Co. Mai was Ba Hai's chief assistant. She was at least in her twenties, and I believe that she was unmarried. She would run things if there were an instance when Ba Hai wasn't there, which wasn't often. Mui Tan would always defer to the Vietnamese women, and seemed to take life in stride.

The detailed company member was more or less along for the ride. They not only took care of themselves, but they took care of the detailed member. Ba Hai and Mai would usually interpret our English to the other detail members, when necessary. They were quite easy to get along with. They were always quite animated and were always talking and laughing with us and at us. Their talk always seemed quite musical.

The highlight of the day was when the waste had to be burned. We teasingly made it a ritual, in which Mui Tan officiated, by throwing in the first match.

The Vietnamese were always very friendly and obliging, and, relations, from my observations, involved mutual respect. They were very passive, and I don't recall any major disagreements with the people, in our company area.

Military rules and regulations and their textbook advocates would rear their ugly heads from time to time, and although, these people had undergone much more scrutiny than the average day-worker, a rule was adopted that required the detailed company member wear side-arms. Although I was aware that you didn't know what to expect from whom, I felt that this measure was totally unnecessary, but I complied. We all would make jokes about it.

One of the more seasoned company members made his statement by having Mai carry the .45, in the holster, over her shoulder. I had a photograph taken of me, on detail with the Vietnamese. The sidearm was turned away from the picture, and the Vietnamese were in the background, in front of the latrine. All of us, to the untrained eye, must have looked extremely dangerous.

Ba Hai was the binding influence in this little band. Mui Tan's manner was traditionally correct, in that he observed the Vietnamese custom of women supervising whatever had to be done to keep a village or area in order. To them this was a woman's domain, and they really didn't tolerate interference. Mui Tan and the detailed members would usually try to avoid being underfoot, and just let them run the show.

I was given to believe that Ba Hai was quite shrewd, and was involved in more than fieldwork, and that she was a madam. Henry Reel, who worked in the motor pool, joked that in about six months, even Ba Hai would look good. Henry, however, was an extreme sort of character who saw sex in everything, and probably could have made Sigmund Freud blush. I kind of wondered how he was going to handle things, psychologically, when he went home, with girls all over the place. I'm reasonably sure that Henry, once back in the world, would have been a psychiatrist' dream come true. I'm reasonably confident that if he survived the trip home, he would probably be either being a politician or a TV minister.

Henry had a hand in an incident that was representative of an altitude that seemed to prevail. On a separate detail, one day, which involved going out of the base camp, he tried to fix me up, at a place that he, and probably everyone else knew about, located not too far from there, in Bac Ha. I refused the offer for two reasons- neither, of which he could understand: The first reason had to do with promises that I made at home, before I left. The other was that Bac Ha, where this thriving business was located, was reported to have a V.C. unit operating in the vicinity. As far as security went, it was just Henry and I and, of course, the ladies, but I don't think they really cared who dropped in. Since I was the only one that I could depend on, I decided that I didn't wish to die like that. I realize that there is probably an element of notoriety, in some quarters, that may invite this happening, but I thought it would be prudent to leave, while we could. I told him things along the lines that we were getting out of there, or I was leaving him behind. It was irrelevant to me that he had the truck, and that I didn't know my way back- but, so what? I did somehow convince him that it was not safe here, without yelling out that there were VC in the area- which I don't think was real news to anybody! What particular words convinced him, to this day, I don't remember, but we did leave, and rather rapidly.

I was well aware that my reaction surprised and hurt Henry, who in his mind was just trying to be hospitable. I'm also sure that he told everyone who would listen, how ungrateful I was. I know this, because, for a long time Top Cook would be grinning at me from ear to ear whenever he saw me. After this, OB reference to an analyst's detection of the "Bac Ha Local Force" would always seem to break the tension in an otherwise serious situation.

On a more serious side I was told by a number of people that this wasn't part of the world and that what we did here didn't matter; nobody would know about it. In many ways I had some problems with that.

Shortly before we left for Xuan Loc Forward, in early November, I did some Christmas shopping of my own, thinking that we were going into a totally different area; I wanted to get some presents to send home. One item that I bought was a straw hat. It was of the type that The Vietnamese wore. This was the only thing that I couldn't ship, because I didn't have anything large enough to ship it in. Just wrapping it in paper wouldn't have worked out, because it would have arrived as a bunch of straw, if it arrived at all. As a parting gift, I gave it to Mui Tan. His hat was in pretty bad shape. I felt that he needed the gift more than anyone at home did. He seemed very grateful. I felt that this was a good opportunity to, not be a tourist, and to make a reasonable contribution without a lot of fanfare. As long as the old hat looked like it had lasted, I'd think that this one is still being used. I liked all of the Vietnamese in that crew. I felt that they were typical of the people here. They were basically farmers, and wanted for very little, except to be left alone. Our presence here wasn't their doing; it wasn't their fault that we were here under these circumstances. Although our presence here brought a prosperity that was never experienced before, it was probably, on the balance, culturally unsettling. They tolerated us, and I'm sure made the best of a bad situation, while we were there. I still hope that God has watched over them, and not let them come to any harm.

25th MIC PERSONALITIES

Some of the personalities that I lived and worked with at Cu Chi, and others, later, at Xuan Loc, are integral to describing the cross-section of class and personality types that made up 25th MIC, and later, 25th MID (584th MID- Xuan Loc Forward). Some were mentioned briefly but these individuals merit describing in more detail.

Larry Moog

Larry Moog arrived in Vietnam about the same time that I did. He was in the first advanced analyst class (RA-1), at Fort Holabird. Larry completed the RA course and came over as a Specialist 5. He was from the St. Paul-Minneapolis area, and had attended the University of Minnesota. He once mentioned that he was there when Hubert Humphrey returned to the University, shortly after he left office. Larry was with me at both Cu Chi and Xuan Loc, and was in the same plane that took us home, in March of the following year. He was with me in both units more time than anyone else was, but I felt that I knew him the least. He was very opinionated, but rarely spoke directly to others. He probably had opinions about me that never came out directly that probably addressed my naiveté', in regard to the overall situation here, in general. His demeanor indicated restraint, which bordered on condescension. He wasn't the sort, however, to openly harass anyone. He had a very dry sense of humor.

He seemed to be an admirer of Winston Churchill and liked to quote him and refer to humorous stories by or about him. Knowing that I liked biographies and histories of the Twentieth Century, He suggested Churchill as a point of reference, on the premise that, like us, he was involved in an increasingly political and unpopular war, but he, none-the-less distinguished himself. I didn't realize then that I was doing my homework for this project.

Larry did his best to make himself at home wherever he was. He liked to relax with a beer and was always the main participant in the bull sessions that ensued, whenever the situation allowed.

Probably, one of the things that he missed most was intelligent conversation. With a relative lack of it in this environment, his general approach to life here was a satirical one, and it was quite amusing, once on his wavelength. I must confess that I was rather intimidated by him, at times, and was always self-conscious of saying something stupid (which I had a lot of practice at) by learning from the experience; I was able to hold my own, in conversation. He was a good teacher. We would talk and have a beer, from time to time. I found out, quite early, however, that I didn't quite have a taste for beer, like he and the others did, and I'd accept the opportunity just for the talk more readily than the beer. The last time I saw him was at Travis Air Force base, when we were going through customs. He never said goodbye, which was quite in character for him. I understood completely. He wasted no time in trying to shed this war. I think of him whenever I see Mark Russell performing, on PBS. His attitude toward the situation seemed to be one of the best ways to psychologically survive the war. I'd be interested to know if he was successful.

Roger Barker

One of the major characters that I was associated with in the 25th MIC was Roger Barker. Roger was in a world of his own, but he made this world interesting enough to encourage investigation of it, looking for lessons for coping with life here. Roger was a very studious character, in spite of his superficial reactions to real-life situations. His college degree was in geology, which was apparently a very valuable asset to the order of battle section. He was from New York, possibly New York City. He liked rodeos, and I was given to believe that he had participated in them. It would seem rather unconventional for someone from that area to have such an interest, but Roger resisted convention as both a hobby and a way of life. He was quite articulate in professional settings, but he was sort of different in every other situation outside of that.

To start with, he wasn't one for good first impressions. He liked to chew tobacco, and he liked to spit it everywhere, at any time. When he was in the shop, however, he was domesticated to the point of using a cup. (Usually his own, but you could never be too sure around him) Sometimes, he would start to spit, sort of hold it in suspension, and then draw it back in. He loved to intimidate newcomers.

His speech patterns were somewhat altered, probably due to the time put in here, and his forced interaction with Army personnel, who had also been here too long. He liked to make monkey sounds, and it was sort of scary- because in a short time I could understand him. It became routine to answer him in his own dialect, and an outsider would have absolutely no idea of what was going on. A low sound, depending on the inflection, could indicate curiosity, agreement or disgust. Louder sounds could be a reaction to Army rules and regulations. This could also be accompanied by facial expressions appropriate to the situation. It was quite an uplifting experience to watch him at work. He was a great showman, and he acted in a style that matched the situation.

Even when we moved to Xuan Loc, Larry and I'd mimic the way that Roger would have responded to a given situation, if he were there. We inherited these sounds, and accordingly tried to pass them on to future generations of intelligence personnel. It didn't make a very good impression with a lot of people in this new setting. Roger's style was also something that couldn't easily be imitated. A lot of people that we worked with felt that was fortunate. Roger went home, around October or November, just before the division stood down. What became of him in the real world can only be guessed. With his broad range of coping mechanisms I think he would have turned out to be quite normal- he just had to get out of here. He kept us laughing and reminded us not to take life too seriously.

Al Hill

Al Hill was another of the more memorable characters that I worked with in the OB shop. When he left in October, I inherited a set of OB files, that he developed- just in time for them to be destroyed. With the Division was standing down, and two brigades returning to Hawaii, most of the files were irrelevant to anywhere else. I did manage to save the parts that would be useful to our new area of operations. Everything else had to be burned.

Al seemed to be quiet and competent, as evidenced by the order of the files. He worked very hard at it, and it showed. I don't think, however, that he would have blocked the destruction of those papers. He probably would have helped to burn them if he weren't so busy packing. I didn't blame him one bit.

John Runnels

John Runnels was from the Detroit area and I remember him mainly for his continuing celebration of his "shortness". It made us all look forward to being in that position.

Tom Scaruzzi

Tom Scaruzzi was from Philadelphia and was an analyst in the order of battle shop, when I first arrived there. He was an easy-going individual, and was of a type who, like Larry Moog, could adapt himself to living anywhere. He was a dark-haired Italian-American, who liked to be the life of the party. He was unpretentious and got along with everyone. He went home about the same time as John Runnels.

Al, Tom and John had spent most of their tour together and got along quite well, but never shut out the new guys like myself. It was as if they had been here forever. From their point of view, it probably felt that was true.

They were all pleasant characters and were great to work with. When they left, there was a major celebration at the Chinese restaurant on another part of Cu Chi base camp. The whole affair was conducted as a roast of the celebrants and we all had a great time. I always hoped that I'd be given a send-off, of that type, when it was time for me to go home. It was something to look forward to.

EDDIE GREEN

Eddie Green was from Baltimore, and was a laid-back individual who was just waiting to go home. I didn't really know him very well, and he didn't talk to me very much. I don't know where he lived in Baltimore; I don't recall asking him. Somehow I didn't feel very much drawn to looking him up, in the states. He seemed to be in another world, long before he left here. In retrospect, if anyone around there could look like he was having a drug problem, it would have been him. I'm not accusing, for I never knew for sure, (nor did I want to know) but I had that feeling. Eddie seemed to have some sort of problem.

A number of films on American servicemen in Vietnam seem to stress the drug problem and how blatantly it was used. In my experience, these depictions were grossly exaggerated. There was drug use, but it was kept very quiet. I wasn't aware of it, except in cases, where individuals would outright insinuate that someone was using something. Eddie seemed to act like that sometimes; but never admitted, nor did I ever see anything being used, in Cu Chi, by members of our unit.

It was continually stressed what some of that stuff did to brain functions, specifically the ability to make rapid and clear judgments and the resulting ability to deal with emergency situations here, rationally. I had no compulsion to do anything like that here, anyway and I had no problem steering clear of that trouble. There were, during the tour, some isolated instances, in which there was peer pressure to participate in such things. It didn't change my feelings toward any sort of drug. I was watching out for me, as best I could.

Jim Macrael

Jim Macrael, the company clerk, was from Salt Lake City. He was, by occupation, a Mormon missionary, and spent a lot of time trying to convert everyone. He was well schooled, but rather programmed- he seemed to depend on memorization of passages from the book of Mormon. This capacity for memorization seemed to be well developed, but he seemed unable to equate what he said in an intelligent discussion of his religion, in comparison to other faiths, particularly Catholicism. Consequently, while he was trying to make me a Mormon, I tried to interest him in becoming a Catholic.

I had little experience in these discussions and wasn't aware that discussions on religion could easily degenerate into a debate. As a result, we both spent a lot of time talking at, rather than to each other. We got along, even though we disagreed on religious grounds. He liked running, as I did, and he showed me the rectangular course along some of the main thoroughfares of the base camp, which he ran regularly. I'd run behind him when time and the situation permitted. I liked getting back to running, once I got used to the climate. I also found that running in the early evening, just before dark, was most comfortable, considering the humidity, here, that we almost constantly had to contend with. After Jim went home, I'd run the course on my own, and eventually showed it to a new-comer, David Neimeyer, who didn't fare too well, in the running department. He decided quickly that he wasn't cutout to be nor did he ever want to be a runner.

Jim was one of the most buttoned-down individuals in the unit. He wasn't, however, a total establishment-type character. He, like others, adapted to the situation. He took criticism well, and never let it deter him from his beliefs. He was mature enough to accept that no one is immune to being laughed at, or criticized for the individual courses that they choose. He was a morally strong individual, in a world where many others preached that this was another planet and positive values brought from home were irrelevant. It was refreshing to know that there were others who trusted in God, even if perceived in another way. I've always hoped that all of us would be right in our perception of God.

Jim, I observed, was highly intelligent, and communicated much better than most of the individuals in the unit. I never really minded his company, even when it did stray into a discussion of Mormonism.

Lt.'s Mitchum and O'Neill

Lieutenants Mitchum and O'Neil were assistants to the section chief Captain Weeks, at 25th MIC OB, and were in charge of the OB section when the 25th MID was in Xuan Loc Forward. They were with me for most of my tour, arriving several months after I did. I group them together to indicate that they usually stuck together, mostly by O'Neil's insistence, rather than Mitchum's. They were both from Georgia- O'Neil from Atlanta, and Mitchum from Monroe. I'm not too sure if O'Neil went to college, but I know that Mitchum had attended Mercer.

They weren't too difficult to get along with. They were young, though several years older than I was. For the most part, they, tactfully, let us be responsible for ourselves. Their requests were usually reasonable; O'Neil, however, was more likely to go over the edge, in insisting on adherence to the military courtesies. Mitchum would at times do so only out of necessity. He could be call up a military bearing when the situation called for it.

O'Neal prided himself on being a true Southerner. Being from Atlanta, he was always singing the praises of their incumbent governor, Jimmy Carter. It was all rather humorous to us-them calling a governor "Jimmi", but he swore by him, and he always took great pains to convince us of all the wonderful things that Carter had done for Georgia. O'Neil's bragging in short order turned us off to all things Georgian, so we never took "Jimmi" too seriously.

J. C. Maguire Jr.

[In 1976, when Carter ran for president, one of his campaign stops was Baltimore, and he made a speech, in Highlandtown, around the corner from where I lived; I immediately liked him. I didn't think his chances were all that great, but I did wish him well. I think that he was the sort of president that was needed for that time. I still believe that the measure of his success was that O'Neil wasn't his public relations man.]

O'Neil wasn't really so bad, but he could be quite changeable, at times. Mitchum had more of a dignity about him, and he could be reasoned with. He even had a sense of humor.

Because of my in-country experience, I had gotten used to the shop routine with Captain Weeks and Mr. Perry. As a result, I, probably subconsciously, always considered them as part of the second team. They probably sensed that; and at times resented that they had to prove themselves competent to an enlisted man. Mitchum seemed more sensitive to this. We had differences of opinion, from time to time, but I feel that we basically were on the same side and understood each other. My candor and seemingly reckless approach to some assignments would sometimes cause some stirs, but he eventually saw them for what they were- ploys for getting input, and he eventually understood and complied.

OTHER PERSONALITIES

Lors Ansel

Lors didn't quite fit one of the categories that I had already laid out, in descriptions of some of the characters. He had a habit of turning up various times and places. Like most of the other individuals that I described, their individual adaptations to life in Vietnam were their trademarks. In his case, he made himself at home in Vietnam. He adapted so completely to the situation that it might have been difficult, if not impossible to be at home back in the states.

I met him early in the tour, when I was still bunked in the transient hootch. He told me that he came over early in the war, probably around 1965. He extended his tour at least four times. There were probably regulations governing this; but, of course, the was a regulation for just about everything, if you went by what the Army approved or disapproved, if one were to approach anything here in a straightforward manner. Transgression of these rules could potentially have ruined the war for everybody. He developed a routine in which he would end his tour, going on R&R, and return for another tour- without ever going back to the U.S. He seemed to love it here. As far as he was concerned, he was home. He made himself so much at home- that he married a Vietnamese, who also wasn't the average Vietnamese female we would likely meet.

I met her on several occasions. She was very attractive, friendly and out-going. She was a soldier and was also much more accomplished than most of her male counterparts. She was assigned to a South Vietnamese Ranger unit. Family life had to be a difficult task to keep up with, under this arrangement, for she had to go where she was assigned. Lors could, by this time, manipulate his assignments so that he could be near her. It seemed to work out quite well. They were a most interesting couple- they even had their occupations in common, although he would never admit to be a career man and had no other lifer-like tendencies that were apparent.

The major complication to their arrangement was they were married by Vietnamese law, but not in an American ceremony. The reason for this was uncertain, but they wanted to correct it. I was honored when he wanted me to be the best man whenever this would come about.

I waited for this, but time didn't seem to mean the same thing to him; I wasn't going to hang around for a couple of tours waiting for this to happen. He showed up several times during the tour, at Cu Chi, and would disappear as fast as he appeared. I'd also hear about him from time to time. I last saw him in Xuan Loc around the end of January, making the same noises.

There is no proper ending to this story, which is par for the course in this overall experience. After I saw him in January, he didn't extend. As I heard it, he went home and got an assignment in Germany- and she wasn't with him.

I don't know what ultimately happened. It seemed to work for them. I couldn't see anything to stop them, considering all that they had been through- except themselves. I grant that there were many things that I wasn't completely aware of. They just seemed to fade into oblivion, kind of like all of us did in our own individual ways.

A Doughnut Dolly

One of the saddest things that I experienced while I was at Cu Chi was the death of a Red Cross volunteer- a Doughnut Dolly. The public face of these ladies involved them in going from unit to unit, talking with the troops, bringing doughnuts, and just being there- in case we forgot what American girls looked like. Circumstantially, I couldn't imagine a place where they wouldn't have been well received.

On the private side, emotional involvement although in one sense, a motivating factor, also had to be an unavoidable hazard. In the case of the woman in question, she obviously made a bad choice and was murdered, presumably by her "boyfriend". At the news of this, a shock wave went through the base camp that couldn't be matched in intensity by incoming artillery. It was such a senseless act.

Apparently, none knew who did it-which technically made everyone a suspect. Each unit was given orders to have all the personnel on the base camp walk through the Red Cross volunteers' quarters. This order had at least a two-fold reason: Foremost, would be that of giving a silent tribute. The other was possibly that the doer of the deed would break down and confess to the crime. This was viewed by many as a futile effort, considering the nature of the military's involvement here. They were looking for a killer among people trained for war.

How this woman died wasn't revealed, nor or any the details given about the investigation. In my researches of 25th Division press releases, at the National Archives sources (NARS) military records, in Suitland, MD. I found nothing about it- not among the items that were released. [Commemorations at the Vietnam Wall, however, did include her.]

The sentiment against whoever did this was very high, and his life probably won't have been worth very much if he were found out. He must have been a very cold-blooded character for it was only much later, when we were in Xuan Loc, that we learned that someone in Headquarters Company was apprehended, and confessed to the murder.

Of all the news that went through the camp and crossed our desks about personnel killed in action or enemy casualty lists, nothing affected all of us, so completely, as the report of this woman's death.

HOME EVENTS

A major means of orientation was the news received from home, from my relatives. I mainly received mail from Betty. My parents and my grandmother would write from time to time, and once, I got a letter from my cousin, Mary Eichelberger. It was always great to get something- anything from home.

In addition to letters that Betty sent she would send cookies and care packages- which contained candy bars, clothes and other odds and ends.

In one instance, I ask her to send for some <u>Old Bay Seasoning</u>, for steaming crabs. These crabs could be bought from a market, near Cu Chi. These were good-sized crabs, which had large claws. When I first had them, we steamed them in beer. I thought that it would be a good idea to send for this seasoning, because I knew how good they would taste. My grandfather had made sure of two things that I should carry on. The first was an enthusiasm for baseball and the other was how to properly steam crabs. As far as he was concerned, these were major Maryland traditions. The seasoning, unfortunately, didn't arrive before I left Cu Chi, and I never got the chance to try it out on those Mekong River crabs. After we had moved to Xuan Loc, I'd ask sometimes about them, but they seemed to be unavailable there. Subsequent inquiries about crabs addressed to non-Maryland GIs were totally misunderstood; which was unfortunate for them too.

The 'Care packages' from home were some of the nicest things that could be received over there, no matter what was in it. We always shared whatever we got in our packages. Some of the things that we got were candy, cheese, cookies or anything else that was edible and could be shipped.

When I left in April, I was married a little more than three months. We also had a child on the way, due in October. I was concerned the whole time about Betty's progress, and wanted, more than anything to be there with her.

I was told by more experienced people that in dealing with women having babies even a combat zone may have been a safer place to be and, if I had to be away, this was the best time for it. My own feelings were that my separation from here was the hardest part of the tour, even of more concern to me than the physical danger. She was and is my best friend, and my life with her was- and is the greatest thing that ever happened to me.

I made a special point of writing as often as I could. Sometimes I'd write two letters a day, if I knew I wouldn't have time to write later, because of bunker guard or any other up-coming event that would keep me from my promise to write at least one letter a day. There were many times that I couldn't write to everyone; so, I'd have Betty relay news to others, in my letters to her.

She would write to me about her visits to the doctor, news from the neighborhood, the garden that she planted, how she missed me, and plans for the future. My not being there was the most painful thing that I experienced, but I knew that this was going to end someday, and at that point, begin a normal life. This was what I hung on to. Instead of concentrating on the negatives, I looked forward to that time. I also talked with her, when I could, on a radio/telephone hook-up, referred to as

MARS- Military Affiliate Radio Station. It was always great to talk to her and my parents. I also got to talk to my grandmother, from time to time.

The communications lag was very frustrating to deal with. It took at least four days for a letter to reach the states, and at least that long to get anything from home. As a result, it was very difficult to get an answer to any timely question, such as paying a bill or any other specific inquiry, for which I needed an immediate answer. The MARS calls were the best ways to deal with situations like this but even this involved an element of luck. Sometimes, the list for these calls was so long that a call may not have been put through, and I'd have to wait for another opportunity. Sometimes, the clarity of the connection left a lot to be desired, and brevity was an important aspect to be observed. The people involved with these radio/telephone hook-ups, however, cannot be given enough credit. Those three minutes with my wife and family were treasured moments, and one of the few links to home. I've always wished that I could have met these people and thank them personally.

There were good and bad times, in which I had no choice, but to deal with from here. One of the saddest involved the death of my grandfather, one of the happiest was the birth my daughter. These were both major events, at that time of my life.

These events occurred fairly close together. My grandfather's death occurred in late September. He was one of the last persons that I said good-bye to, when I left for Vietnam, the previous April. Of all the people, that I said good-bye to, he was rather different. The words were irrelevant; there was a look in his eyes that I never saw in anyone else's. It gave me the feeling that we weren't going to see each other again. Considering where I was going, I felt that my chances were just as good as his, that I'd be the one. I didn't want to be negative; I wanted to be strong. I'm not sure how I did. For his part, knowing my grandfather, like I did, I knew that he could get quite emotional- and still deny it. My brother Pat is like that, and could be caught many times, crying at the end of a sad movie, and hiding it. I felt that my grandfather was on the verge of that. I reassured him that I was coming back. I wanted really badly for him to be there when I returned.

On a late September night, In Cu Chi, I finished what I felt was a regular work day, and tried to relax for the night. For some reason, I couldn't. I read, went to the E.M. club, walked around and talked to anyone who was still awake. I never before had any trouble sleeping, when I was on this tour. Something was wrong- I could feel it, but I didn't know what. I wandered over to the OB shop, just out of curiosity, to see if anything was going on; everything was quiet. The only things going on were routine, such as Joe Sneed having taken his pillow out of his file cabinet, settling down for the night. I finally went back to the OB hootch, and fell asleep reading a James Bond novel, about 4:30 or 5:00 A.M., just before it was time to get up.

When I did get up, I got word that I was to contact the Red Cross. Something had happened at home. I thought that the baby might have arrived. I hoped that everything was all right. When I did call, I was told that my grandfather had died, and that I should arrange a priority MARS call home and talk to my parents.

I spent the entire day, examining my options. This included leaving at a particularly bad time. Even if the C.O. granted it, the time element involved in returning to Vietnam would cause me to forsake military hops, resorting to commercial air travel, which I couldn't afford. I wanted to be home, but there was little that I could do. I talked to my father, later that day, and he agreed, saying basically the same thing that the Major Fitzgerald had told me. By the time that I'd have arrived, the funeral would be over. I felt helpless to do anything, frustrated that I couldn't be with my family at this time. It brought back again, just how much I missed home. It also caused me to remember the good things about my grandfather, and the life that he enjoyed. It wasn't a materially rich life, but he had the things that counted, and I know that he wanted them for all of us. He was the only one, who really pushed college, although he didn't attend past Baltimore's Polytechnic Institute. He gave a lot of advice that people my age didn't see the sense of following; but he still tried! I'll always appreciate that.

He was anxious for his first great grandchild to be born. He came within about a month of having that come true. This event prompted some of the saddest letters that I was to write from Vietnam, to my grandmother. I did resolve that he loved, in his life, sports, and looking on the light side of things. For that, his life was a happy one, and I was glad for that.

When Larry Moog, and the others, had approached me, offering their condolences, I feel that I might have seemed insensitive to the whole thing. I had half-expected that this was going to happen, and I also knew that I won't know how to handle it, whenever it happened. I did appreciate their concern; but I felt kind of lost for a while.

I'll always wonder how I knew that something had happened, at the same time that it happened, from 12,000 miles away. There is no logical way that I could have known, but I felt it. I'm somewhat neutral, in regards to things paranormal, but several things, like that, made me wonder. In another instance, I had similar feelings, on what turned out to be a much happier occasion.

By the beginning of October, it was clear that the 25th Division would be standing down; sending two of its brigades back to Hawaii. All of us dreamed that on account of this we might all be going home. Realistically, I knew that it wasn't likely to happen to me. I had only six months in country and early-outs were granted to individuals who were much closer to going ending their regular tour. Plans were still in the works, and it seemed, most likely, that I'd be staying behind, with the Second Brigade, which was moving to Xuan Loc., located about forty miles northeast of Saigon. At least, I'd be staying with the 25th Division, and people that I knew. That was my only consolation.

My real concern, at this time, was my proximity to a means of communication, to contact home. The baby was due, at any time after the middle of October. I was starting to exhibit every sign of becoming a nervous father; all of my letters indicated that. I called at least twice a week, or more, if I could get on the list, for the MARS calls. I was continually reassured that Red Cross would notify me when anything happened; they would find me, wherever I was. All I could do was wait. (And wait...and wait...) I even bought cigars (And I don't smoke).

A stand-down party was organized with the Headquarters Company, and preparations were made to make it a really big celebration. It was held, coincidentally, on the 25th of October. There was food, music, beer, and all sorts of other things to celebrate the departure of the division for Hawaii. It was all very nice, but I had this feeling...

This was an all-day celebration, and it took most of the day to set up. While this was going on, I called to get on the list for the MARS calls, for that evening. I had called a few days before, but Betty was still waiting, too. I made up my mind, that I was going to call, whenever the opportunity presented itself- and it did that night. All that night, I went back and forth between the party and the wardroom. Amidst music, circus acts, beer and Vietnamese dancing girls, I waited for word from home. My only suffering was in waiting for that call. It seemed to take forever. It may be that nothing happened yet, I thought; but maybe it did.

At about 10:30, I got word that my call was about to be put through. I went to the OB shop, and called the MARS people, so they would connect me. When the call did go through, my father answered. Betty wasn't there... because she had the baby, about four hours before! I was told that I had a daughter, weighing in at eight pounds, twelve ounces. Betty and I agreed, in advance, that if the baby was a girl, we would call her Linda Ann. My father did get to tell me that both were doing fine, before the three minutes were up. As the call was ending, another voice came on the line, saying that they were calling the hospital, to attempt to contact Betty.

As I was waiting for the call to go through, Sergeant Michalic, who happened to be there that night, had surmised what had happened; and he and the others were grinning from ear to ear. I guess that all of us, here, were, in our own ways, pacing the floors, before this, and they were at least as glad as I was that this was over-partly, because I could finally break open that can of cigars that I was saving! I believe that Sergeant Michalic got the first one.

When the connection to Bon Secours Hospital was finally made, the nursing staff on the floor made Betty available almost immediately. I didn't know it at the time, but they pushed the bed out into the hall, and picked up the baby, on the way. Betty told me that she and the baby were all right. I know that my father had already told me, but it was even nicer hearing it from her. She sounded pretty tired, but happy. She told me that she was holding the baby, and wanted to hold her up to the receiver, so that I could hear her. One of the nurses had pinched her toe, and she started crying, very loudly. There was definitely nothing wrong with her lungs. It sounded like she wanted everybody to know that she had arrived. In this manner, I heard her for the first time, halfway around the world. It was an incredible feeling. I was really beyond words. Of course, she had to be prompted, to make any noise, but she has had no trouble verbalizing ever since. I always tease her about the difficulty in getting her off the phone, now!

I did get to tell Betty how much I love her, and how proud I was of her. All too soon, the time was up, and I had to say good-by. Before I hung up, I tried to thank the people who made the MARS hook-ups possible, but they were already off helping someone else. I'll never forget them. Those calls meant a lot to me.

The official word came down that the staff had been picked for the Second Brigade's intelligence detachment, and I'd be with that unit in Xuan Loc Forward. What would be considered Xuan Loc Rear would be located at Camp Frenzel-Jones, in Long Binh. The company, by this time was in the process of packing up and leaving Cu Chi to the South Vietnamese Army's, 25th ARVN.

We were on duty, through the first week of November, dismantling the shop, and burning files that wouldn't be needed, in our new area of operations.

With the departure of the main elements of the 25th Division, one of the largest base camps in South Vietnam was being turned over to the South Vietnamese armed forces, apparently to point out that Vietnamization was working. I wasn't completely sure that it was; but this is what they were telling us.

One of the last details involving the 25th MIC here was in response to threats of a sapper attack. Sappers were the demolitions experts and specialized in mines, bangalore torpedoes and anything involving a bomb or a booby trap. Harassment of withdrawing units was just one of their specialties. This was one of the things to be anticipated in such an operation. Apparently, it wouldn't be good enough for the NVA and the local VC to just watch us leave and be done with it. Apparently, it was important to them to be able to make the local inhabitants believe that they had driven us out; hence, the heightened expectations of a sapper attack. At the time, in this area of operations, little could have been done by the NVA to launch a major attack on Cu Chi. Any elements that were capable of that were driven deep into Cambodia, and their staging areas were decimated. The ARVNs were also conducting continuous cross-border operations, which also served to keep the NVA off-balance.

Any operation against Cu Chi would have been an isolated one- with no coordination of other elements. We did receive a 122mm rocket that exploded harmlessly in an unpopulated area of the camp- otherwise it was quiet.

The 25th MIC was detailed at the gate, with the MPs, checking vehicles and people, going in and out, checking for weapons and infiltrators. I never realized the extent of the vehicle and people traffic, in and out of the main gate. Up till that time, I never saw a lot of Vietnamese day workers. There must have, easily, been a thousand of them- all trying to get checked out at the same time. It looked like the proverbial Chinese fire drill.

We alternated between looking at vehicles, and the people going out. The personnel in military vehicles resented being checked, and we had to take it. It was better to do this than to have something worse happen. We got through the detail without incident. The division finally stood down, and we were on our way to Xuan Loc, by the second week of November.

CU CHI SUMMARY

In attempting to describe the atmosphere of Cu Chi, there may be a lot that I missed. My view of it was as an enlisted man, in a military intelligence company, which was involved in some major operations. Life here was hardly home, nor was it as described by disinterested civilians or by most Holabird instructors. Very little of what I was told at Fort Holabird really applied here, except for the briefings on Russian and Chinese weaponry, and the classes on the types of American units we would be in liaison with, as a military intelligence unit.

One briefer at Holabird had mentioned Cu Chi, describing it as one of the better places to be in Vietnam. From what I heard of other places I agree with that assessment. Another factor may have been that it was a completely American unit. An assignment with the 25th Infantry Division didn't have the complication of being directly involved with the Military Assistance Command for Vietnam (MACV). Administratively, it was under United States Army, Vietnam (USARV). Having relatively little knowledge of MACV versus USARV, I don't feel that I've the information to do a fair comparison of these commands. Both probably had their own problems to deal with in doing their job. From my point of view, functioning with an American unit, under American control, was preferred as a more familiar and adaptable situation.

During the time that I was in Cu Chi, I had the opportunity to record this experience in many ways- by letters, photographs, tape recordings, and my own memory. This was exclusive of the paper that a unit like this would have generated, and whatever else is available to researchers at the Army Archives, at Carlisle, Pennsylvania, and at the previously-mentioned National Archives Repository in Suitland, Maryland.

One of the more notable things that the archives may record is a visit, to Cu Chi, by The Commander of the American Armed Forces, in Vietnam, General Creighton Abrams. He officiated in a ceremony, in which a unit citation was awarded to the Third Battalion of the Fourth Cavalry Regiment, nick-named 'Three-Quarter Cav' This was the most elaborate ceremony that I was to witness, while I was in Vietnam. The divisional formation was complete with all the pomp and circumstance that could be mustered, in that particular area.

I took some photographs and made a tape recording of the ceremony. These items are still in my possession. The photos are in good condition, but the recording is of poor quality, due to some technical problems that I had with the recorder. My nearness to the public address system may have also accounted for this. These items may be valuable additions to Army archives. I hope, someday, to make it a gift to them.

In the seven months that I lived on Cu Chi base camp, I had come to regard it, in a twisted sort of way, as home. A change in assignment, would be, in effect, starting all over again. I felt that I was fortunate, that I'd be staying with the 25th Division, even though I wasn't too sure what I was in for. I was to find out fairly soon, just how much of a change I was in for.

PART III- XUAN LOC

The Journey

In early November, all preparations were made, for the 25th to re-deploy. As a member of the newly designated 25th MID, I was busy packing up and getting ready for another bout with the unknown. My concerns were real enough; this brigade would have about only one-third of the size and strength of a full division. Security in the surrounding area would also be a totally different arrangement. As an extra added measure, the 25th MID would be split up into forward and rear elements. As a subordinate unit of II Field force (Second Field Force), in Long Binh, the forward detachment would be in one of the two 2/25th compounds in Xuan Loc, and the rear elements would be located in Camp Frenzel Jones, in Long Binh.

In terms of order of battle, I had little knowledge of what was going on in that area. I did know that we would be depending on 18th ARVN Division (Army Republic of Vietnam), for support in area defense. Our compound was located about a half-mile from a MACV compound. We also shared one of the two compounds, at Xuan Loc Forward with an Australian unit.

Some of the personnel that were to make up 25th MIC had already left Cu Chi by the end of October, to help set up the MID. We were kept informed of their progress, at least every few days. They even acquired a mascot.

By the time the rest of the detachment was ready to arrive, the billets and the section shops were set up for us on the compound. We left Cu Chi, for the last time in the second week of November.

Everything that I had acquired, in the last seven months had to be packed up. I was amazed at the amount of material I had collected in that relatively short amount of time; I had <u>really</u> moved in. I guess this a universal complaint of anyone who has to move anywhere. I just never realized just how much I had made myself at home here. I had a bunk, table, standing locker, footlocker, lamp, clothes, weapon and all sorts of miscellaneous odds and ends. My apprehension dissipated as my attention was turned to having to move all these things to our next place of residence.

All transportation, for this move, was by jeep and truck. This was the most I had seen, at this point, of the Vietnamese countryside. Most of my time at Cu Chi had been spent on the base camp. It was a fairly uneventful trip, but it was very scenic and a most interesting ride.

After traveling from Cu Chi, along Highways 7, and 13, we made one stop in Long Binh, at what was to be Xuan Loc Rear, located in Camp Frenzel Jones. The main building of a very small compound, which reminded me of an icehouse; it had quite a large door in the back, probably for use as a loading dock. It was one of the fortunes of war, in that buildings assigned to us were not custom-made. We basically took what we got. It was a novelty, to have such a door on that building. I couldn't think of what possible use it would have for us. This building was to be used for imagery interpretation, the interrogation section and probably some elements of counterintelligence. Xuan Loc Forward would have basically the same elements, in addition to order of battle, and we would be a lot closer to what was going on.

A Contradiction of Terms: A 25th Division Analyst's Tour in Vietnam

The complex at Long Binh was so massive and sprawling; that it enclosed what had been at least several small villages and at least one cemetery, which was adjacent to the Frenzel Jones compound. We would be more involved here, as the MID was activated.

We proceeded to Xuan Loc, along Route One. We had been traveling, for most of the trip on Highway 13, all the way from Cu Chi. Highway 13 was an asphalt-topped secondary road, which wound through the countryside, in a general east-west direction, from At least Long Binh to the Cambodian border. Route 1, however, was vastly different from anything that I had seen here, up to that time. It was as wide, and as busy as any of the major highways, back in Maryland. It reminded me of Ritchie Highway- without the hamburger stands and the drive-ins. It was the most traffic that I had seen since I had arrived in Vietnam.

A large percentage of the vehicles other than military, were also buses, Lambretta trucks (modified golf carts or motorized rickshaws), and motorcycles- mostly Hondas. It was quite a change from the country roads that we previously traveled. These roads were made of concrete. As out-of-place, as it seemed, they were necessary for an area so close to the Long Binh complex, which in many places, didn't look like part of Vietnam. We stayed on this highway, until we were near Xuan Loc.

As we traveled east, we passed Bien Hoa City, a beautiful little Oriental town, which looked rather untouched by the war. Located near Cholon, it was probably considered to be in the eastern suburbs of Saigon- not too far from here was the air base from which I started my tour and hoped to leave from there, as soon as possible. As we traveled east, the terrain changed from vast expanses of bare, flat lands, to long rolling hills and trees, and assorted jungle vegetation on both sides. These areas were cleared back, at least a hundred feet, probably to reduce cover, in the event of any attempt to interdict the highway.

At one point, one top of a hill was a mansion, which seemed to be a reminder of the past French presence here- a historical reminder of people who have come and gone, over the years. I had no knowledge of the area, and what it had been or was being used for then. It quite possibly could have been a school. This mansion seemed to stand alone, among the trees. There was nothing else around it.

We then passed two areas along Route One, which were probably major markets in the region. The whole area east of Saigon seemed to be much more fertile and conducive to vegetable farming, than the area to the West. Trang Bang and Trang Baum were the major centers from which area farmers sold their goods. Trang Baum was, probably, the more formal marketing area. It was highlighted by a large open-air building, made of stone, and seemed to draw a large number of local residents to its center. Trang Bang was a smaller marketplace, looking more like an oversized farmer's market, similar to the ones back home.

Further down the road, we crossed a bridge, which was heavily guarded by South Vietnamese regional forces. This small bridge was made to look very important, judging from the number of men guarding it. It looked as if they had had trouble with the VC and NVA very recently.

We passed two churches along the way. The first was a Catholic Church. A photo that I took of it shows the church, itself, and the area around it. On other trips to and from Long Binh, we saw children playing outside in the schoolyard. The other church was a Buddhist temple. The temple was very colorful, and was covered with various symbols of Buddha, including one, that, in Western cultures could be taken for a swastika. Both places were empty, when we passed them on that particular day.

All along the roadside, coming from no place in particular, children would appear, making peace signs and smiling. Major Moore, on subsequent trips, would bring along candy, to throw to them, as we went by. They were always friendly, and they certainly appreciated the candy.

As we neared Xuan Loc, there was a wooden post, marked XA Xuan Loc, indicating the district and, not too far away, the city with the same name. Xuan Loc wasn't so much a city at all; it could have passed for a small American town, except for the military vehicle traffic, and the Vietnamese faces. It wasn't a densely populated area, and it was well kept. One of the major reasons for this was that it was off-limits to American personnel, at night. A past incident involving a GI and a Vietnamese officer's wife had apparently led to some altercations.

On entering Xuan Loc City, we passed the MACV compound, which was located just a half-mile from the compound that we would occupy. The main features of the MACV compound were a PX, a steak house and a gift shop. The compound was entirely enclosed. The wooden structures within were very solidly constructed. Along the structures were wooden planks, which were also, built very strongly- not just laid down in a temporarily. The structures in the main area had large wooden awnings that extended over the planks, resembling the style that is seen in westerns, on which the cowboys would walk, after tethering up their horses and going to the nearest saloon. It seemed to have that sort of atmosphere. It was all very well kept. I'm not entirely sure of what administrative or strategic function the MACV compound served, but it was a nice place to visit, especially after we had been on our own compound for a while.

After passing the MACV compound, we turned left, onto a dirt road, and went the half-mile to our compound. It was rather small, compared to Cu Chi, and it was nowhere near as elaborate as the MACV compound that we had just passed. The perimeter of the compound was composed mostly of chain-link fencing and barbed wire.

The bunkers on the entrance side of the compound were of two basic sizes. On the corners, they were about twenty feet high and resembled the towers at Cu Chi. The bunkers on the sides were much closer to the ground, and heavily sandbagged.

As we turned right and entered the gate, I tried on the idea of calling this place home. It didn't seem as bad as it was made out to be. It looked Spartan, but peaceful. My apprehensions somewhat mellowed by then. The entrance to the compound was a simple chain-link gate, similar to Cu Chi, but without the elaborate MP contingent. Here, only about one or two MPs at a time would be at the gate.

The compound was small, compared to Cu Chi. While entering the front gate, the back gate, about three or four blocks away, could be seen directly opposite. A fairly large mountain, Nui Choi Chan, could be seen, about ten miles distant. The motor pool was on the right, and the enlisted men's club was next to that. To the left of the main roadway, were the barracks buildings for the 65th Engineers. Behind these, were our barracks buildings; this would be where we would be living. There was a concrete walkway from the main road leading all the way back to our quarters for the 25th

MID enlisted. The buildings were constructed of pre-fabricated metal with concrete floors, with a set of double doors on each side.

The compound itself looked relatively undisturbed. Unofficial reports of trouble were grossly exaggerated. The concrete walkways were not new; they looked as though they had been there for a long time. If any part of the compound took a mortaring, it wasn't here; it was a fairly well-kept area, and nowhere near as compressed as our quarters at Cu Chi.

When we entered the building assigned to OB, and some of the other sections, we were told to stake out our own areas. I picked the corner on the right side nearest the doorway.

The compound itself was unlike anything that we had been accustomed to. In contrast to Cu Chi's, MIC compound, which was essentially barren of vegetation, this compound had many large trees. On the southern part of the compound, were large groves. In general, the area was neatly kept, with a fairly elaborate system of intersecting dirt roads and walkways, giving access to an interesting mix of aluminum and wooden buildings.

The order of battle shop occupied a third of a long wooden building nearest to the southern perimeter. The OB shop was located in the same building as the S2, almost in the exact opposite corner of the compound.

The location of this building left a lot to be desired. The screening of the building, also, was in disrepair; and until it was paid attention to, we would be at the mercy of the many types of flying insects, especially in the evening. We were also in proximity to a very large artillery piece, probably a 155mm Howitzer that shook the ground and everything else around it when it was fired.

We were also situated about 200 meters from a chopper pad. Almost continually, there were noises associated with the comings and goings of the Hueys, light observation helicopters (LOHs- pronounced loaches) and Cobra gunships, which continually landed and took off, from the compound. The noises were eventually taken for granted. After a while, we came to accept it just a way of life in the area.

Xuan Loc forward was divided into two compounds; the other was less than a mile away, to the north. I only saw it, on one occasion. None of the MID units were located here, and, not until later, did I know that it was called Husky Compound. For our compound, only our unit designations were used as identifying characteristics; and the Xuan Loc Forward was the only name that I recall was used.

The weather here seemed quite moderate. It was hot, but with the trees and other vegetation, which afforded shade that was almost non-existent in Cu Chi, it was quite tolerable. The temperature itself seldom got very cool, but after so many months, when sleeping without a fan was torturous, it was quite comfortable. The area looked well irrigated, in contrast to areas West of Saigon, where the area was more suitable for rice farming. This region seemed to be an area that was most suitable to vegetable farming.

The long trip from the region west of Saigon was over. This would be where we would be hanging our hats for the next four months. It was like starting all over again.

We were in an area that we knew relatively little about. This was another venture into the unknown. Throughout my tour, every place that I was stationed in Vietnam had unique characteristics, which very effectively represented the cultural diversity of Vietnam; Xuan Loc would be no exception.

XUAN LOC PERSONALITIES

The situation in Xuan Loc seemed to have all the ingredients for a play, in this cast of characters: Henry---, Neal---, Mr. Brown, Frank Croty, Frank Canoly, David Neimyer, Will Guhman, Lieutenants. Mitchum & O'Neill, Major Pattison, Col. Ulatowski, Terry Herweh, Jim Maddox, Mark Richardson, Ba One, Mae, Hue, assorted members of bunker detail, engineers, ARVNs, Thais, Australians, Lors Ansel, Admiral John S. McCain, Hoi Chanhs, USO personnel, indigenous Saigonese, Xuan Loc City residents, assorted Vietnamese along Route One, National Police, regional and provincial forces

David Neimyer

David Neimyer was from St. Louis. He was a product of Fort Holabird and of 70-RA-3, the advanced analyst class. He was a somewhat nervous personality who exhibited an attitude of continual disgust and sarcasm, in regard to most matters. For the most part, this was just an act, and he operated most of the time with a well-disguised good humor. Although, he would never admit it, he was one of the more personable characters in the unit. He would good-naturedly flaunt his St. Louis/German background, and their circumstantial beer-drinking habits. He would pal around with Will Guhman, who was also in the same rotation at Holabird.

David had a somewhat adventurous personality, in a cautious sort of way; in that, he would try anything once. Fortunately, he usually experimented on the side of relatively harmless undertakings like running, chess and beer drinking. He only seemed generally successful with the latter. He was terrible at both running and chess, but I do give him credit for, at least, trying. From the start, it was determined that he wasn't a runner. He barely survived the basic course, around the blacktop of the Cu Chi base camp. I had to alternately push him and pull him through the course before he finally quit.

David was, by nature, argumentative, and would constantly play devil's advocate in discussing any given subject. His likeability had to do with his not taking himself too seriously. He would many times take an outrageous stand on some topic of current import, after finding out how everyone else stood on it. He would occasionally get serious; at least enough to show that he was concerned and as scared as everyone else around here was. He looked forward to a career as a muckraker, but I think that, for what he had in mind, in the context of Vietnam, Daniel Ellsberg beat him to it.

He would practice incessantly, in his spare time, on the basketball court, next to the shop. He taunted me into improving my free throw ability, and was partially responsible for continuing to improve on my ability to shoot from mid-court.

David and I'd always be bantering about one thing or another, and Lt. Mitchum would usually react as if we never got along with each other and would berate us with regularity. In reality, nothing could have been further from the truth. The tone of our dialogue served to keep us sane.

Will Guhman

Will Guhman was another product of 70-RA-3. He was a tall, light-haired character, with a square jaw and rough appearance, which he, many times, played up for effect. He had a fondness for doing impressions of former instructors and of doing impressions of commentators, and their descriptions of the war. One of the impressions that he did best was of the old marine instructor at Holabird, Gunny Harker, one of our all-time favorites. Gunny's unique style, as well as his own personal opinions about the conduct of the war, had made a lasting impression on the R and RA classes at the time. Because Will did this impression so well, he was nicknamed "Gunny." He liked it, and it stuck.

His other major impression involved a commentator, probably of his own invention, who sounded vaguely like racecar driver Jackie Stewart, describing a human wave attack, sounding something along the lines of: "the yellow divels...herling thimselves ore' the barbed wire..."

He must have remembered every instructor that he ever had any contact with, for he continuously would lampoon them. He had to be the MID's equivalent to Roger Barker, although, I doubt that anyone could have even thought about topping Roger. Will was the closest.

Frank Croty

Frank Croty was the principal interrogator involved with us at Xuan Loc Forward. All members of this section, by the nature of the job, had to travel a lot, and out of necessity, work out of Frenzel-Jones. Frank was in Xuan Loc from the start of operations here. He was married, and one of the few who understood what I was going through, in missing my wife. He would remind me that it would be worth the wait, and that I could look her and everyone in the eye, in saying that I was true to my word.

Major Pattison

Major Jack Pattison wasn't directly a member of the 25th MID, but his description is vital, in order to set the tone for some of the operations that were involved in getting through this part of the tour, in Xuan Loc. He was in charge of S2 brigade-level intelligence matters. He was referred to, as with others in similar positions, (among other things) as the S2. The most distinct memory of the major was that he had absolutely no sense of humor. Granting that war is a serious business, and no laughing matter, I couldn't help, in that regard, agreeing with the major; however, this man seemed totally devoid of a lighter side.

Confrontations with him were not to be relished. My one major encounter with him really left me wondering if he had absorbed any of the jargon that was routinely used around the shop, to describe operations. A report that I handed him, in response to an inquiry, had to be typed, and even then, it wasn't likely that he would be pleased with it. I later found that my experience with him was comparable to what others had gone through routinely. He came to be referred to as "Smiling Jack" - because he rarely, if ever did. He seldom spoke directly to order of battle personnel, and more often than not, we would hear from him through his chief NCO. This would only happen when he felt that there was something that we should know. The concept of need to know was extended to the limit. This was quite difficult to maintain, since the S2 section was adjacent to the OB section, just over a four-foot high partition. As a consequence, we had to keep our comments to ourselves. Audible communication was usually put on hold, till either the shop was empty, we could talk outside, out of earshot or were off-duty, when it did absolutely no good at all, in getting the job done. Audible communications seemed to highly agitate him, although most of our business was conducted with continuous takeoffs and landings of the choppers and the periodic shaking of the S2 building by a nearby battery of 155s. The operational situation, in Xuan Loc was just another instance of the environment, which we were supposed to adjust to, for the sake of getting the job done. The major, in many instances personified these paradoxes.

Before leaving Cu Chi, I talked with another analyst, who was on his way home. He had a lot of experience at brigade level, S2, as well as division level, G2. On the several occasions that we did get to talk, he gave me some very useful advice in understanding and dealing with them. Some of this advice had to do with observing their reactions under certain conditions, in order to determine if I was being lied to. The main point of these tips served to remind us that we were just along for the ride, and nothing I could do was going to get me back home, in one piece, any faster.

As our operations in Xuan Loc became more set, I could almost hear this guy laughing at me saying that he told me so. Lt. Mitchum would routinely limit our discussion, and all noise that would emanate from our section of the S2. As section chief, he was especially under the Major's scrutiny, and as a result, had to accede to his wishes, and as the children we were, we were apparently supposed to be seen and not heard, unless spoken to. Our process of audibly hammering out our solutions seemed to greatly irritate him. He was just interested in the results. We had little privacy, however, to do that.

The gap between what Mitchum knew and what he was telling us was considerable enough to cause tension among us, from time to time. I really wanted to help. I needed to be doing something positive, and was continually frustrated from making that contribution. The work eventually became secondary to my personal writings and after-hours routine and details.

In surviving this tour psychologically, I noticed that I was adapting a rather unmilitary attitude. There were always subtle reminders that I was still in the Army, whenever I'd stray too far off the mark, which happened periodically. We developed a manner, which involved dealing with issues in a half-joking way, usually under our breaths, inaudible to the higher-ranking individuals, who had to take this far more seriously. The balance of this was that we could hate it all we wanted, but as long as the military courtesies were maintained, there were no real problems.

The most blatant reminders were gotten from Major Pattison, who didn't have a remnant of a sense of humor. I'd just as soon rather forget some of these quasi-confrontations. His lack of a lighter side, however, was a constant stimulus and a major source of mirth, within our section.

Other Sections

Most of the personnel and equipment associated with the Imagery Interpretation section was located at Frenzel-Jones. Usually, our only contact with them was, in addition to normal liaison with Xuan Loc Rear and in reports that were found in the Intsums from II Field Force, in Long Binh. The personnel were, at this point in time, usually nameless, and we hardly met them face to face. The situation changed, when we arrived in Long Binh, in March, to stand down.

In the CI Section, Mr. Brown and Neil Hill came over from the 25th MIC. There were others in the section, but they probably worked out of Frenzel-Jones, along with interrogation and Imagery Interpretation sections. For the most part, they kept to themselves, as if to add to the mystique of counterintelligence. Mr. Brown and Neil were easy to get along with, and not standoffish, as were others in that section who, by nature, came off as prima donnas.

XUAN LOC ROUTINE

Life on the Xuan Loc compound was somewhat comfortable, once a routine was established. Our living quarters were more or less run by an elderly Vietnamese lady, with the assistance of several young girls. She had to be quite capable, for she had to keep an eye on our hootches and the girls at the same time. The situation itself shows some of the marked contrasts between Eastern and Western cultures. The girls were always obedient to Ba One, although it was always evident that she had her hands full. Most probably, her secret of success was that she quietly kept all of us in line. Her manner was never blatantly domineering, but she elicited respect from all of us. She always mothered the girls and us at the same time. She had a tremendous sense of humor, and was always quick with an appropriate comment to lighten the day. With us around, I'm sure that she always had a lot to laugh about. When American words failed her, her niece, Hue, would translate the Vietnamese for us. Whatever may have been lost in the translation was made up for by Hue's manner, which was a balance between respect for us and Ba One and the apparently outrageous comments that of her aunt would impart.

The situation here was similar to that of Cu Chi, in respect to the Vietnamese workers. Here the positions were more refined, and the Vietnamese that we were in contact with were involved in housekeeping. The mess hall employed a fair number of the local Vietnamese, and some were involved in serving the Non-coms, at their tables. The food wasn't especially good, but the service balanced it out.

Laundry was done daily, except on Sundays, and the group would always be there early and on time. If one of us pulled night duty, they usually worked around us, as long as we didn't willfully get underfoot. During the day, this was their domain, and we were tolerated with skill and diplomacy that would have changed history if it had implemented at a higher level.

One improvement of this compound over our quarters at Cu Chi is that, here, we had hot water. Showers were a lot more comfortable, and clothes were easier to wash. Even though this compound was in a much more rural area, we had a luxury that we didn't have before. In Cu Chi, we had to take showers from water stored in what looked like torpedo tubes mounted on top of the shower house. If the sun beat down on them, as it usually did, a shower in the early evening wasn't so bad. If the sun didn't shine for a few days, especially during the monsoon seasons, showers were more than a little bit bracing. If one would come back to the compound after an evening of bunker guard, especially after the water truck had just replenished the tubes during the night, showers tended to be very quick ones. On this compound, the only hazard involved getting to the showers in the morning, before the Vietnamese girls started using it as another place to do the laundry. A late morning shower could be rather embarrassing.

The compound, though relatively small, was, once fully manned, very busy. In addition to our unit was a detachment of engineers, Australian liaisons, a communications unit with a large radio tower, a battery of 155mm artillery, and a helicopter pad, which was in constant use. There was also a chapel, enlisted men's club and a metal container that was our post office.

In contrast to the Cu Chi base camp, this compound was in a grove of trees, which afforded much more shade than we had been accustomed to in our other place of residence. It was quite comfortable. Always mindful that this was still in a war zone, and all things being relative, it was tolerable. For now it was home, and we adapted to it quite well.

The only major detail that had to be attended to was bunker guard. On our compound, perimeter security was a much more personal matter; for 25th MID personnel generally got the assignment closest to our quarters, which bordered on the main road, facing the gate. From here, all the comforts of home were fairly close at hand; and the only inconvenience was staying up all night.

2/25TH DIVISION OPERATIONS

One interesting aspect of the Vietnam War was the use of sophisticated means of communication, by all parties involved. The paradox was that the people on the outside of the situation knew a whole lot more of what was going on here than we did- or at least had access to it. The same pertains to freedom of movement, as I shall later illustrate. It's of great significance that, aside from individuals, each group had its own independent criteria for reality, and what was necessary to maintain it. The universal concern, fear of death, and was a constant in shaping one's personal view.

To a politician or a high-level military strategist, I perceive that reports of casualties on both sides, was subordinated by strategic results of execution of a major operation, and the long-term formulation of foreign policy. I also perceive that face-saving was also their major preoccupation, on both sides of the battle lines.

My personal perceptions were obtained from official reports from our side, which described how well we were winning the war and that our troop withdrawals were proceeding as planned- or ahead of schedule. This withdraw schedule, however, didn't seem to have much of a bearing on when I'd be going home. There always seemed to be something hollow about these pronouncements because I was still there- 12,000 miles from home. Official reports obtained from captured VC and NVA documents said, in essence, that things were going well for their side; and, that the Americans and those who assisted the anti-Communists would soon be driven from Vietnam. It didn't seem relevant that the Americans were leaving Vietnam, anyway. It was probably important to them that they take credit for something that Americans at home decided on their own. With such glowing reports emanating from both sides, things were going along just fine. As far as waging a war was concerned, who could ask for anything more? It was difficult to ascertain just who was telling the truth, and who really had the upper hand. If anything was obvious at all, the real losers were the people of Vietnam, who really wanted to be and should have been, left alone.

What was really going on in the upper echelons could only be guessed at. Both sides, by this time had already passed the point of unwilling and were unable to affect a peaceful solution. The attempts to solve it had degenerated into forums to tell the world how wrong each side was. The negotiations were a facade, designed to give the world a feeling that things were in the process of being worked out, while each side was going to do whatever they had planned to in the first place. At this point in time, I knew how it was going to end. Both sides were ultimately unwilling to solve the inherent problems. As an individual, I feel that I was just (again) along for the ride.

At this level, in my own situation, I dealt with individuals who were unwilling to mouth what was obvious: we could stay here, for as long as Americans could afford it. When we left, there was a high degree of certainty that the GVN would lose their country to the Communists. From the time that I arrived in Xuan Loc, I knew how it was going to end. I didn't know when; and I hoped that I wouldn't be here to see it happen. Believing that this was bound to happen, the situation dictated that the best I could do here would be to get out of here in one piece and tell what I had seen and experienced. What I didn't count on was that the people at home were, despite all their sophisticated communications means, not listening. They had long since ideologically washed their hands of the Vietnamese people and of any fellow Americans who came to assist them. In my early experience, of returning home, no one wanted to know what it was really like to be here. If someone did venture to ask, interest would quickly wane, as soon as my descriptions of Vietnam interfered with how they already perceived it to be. It seemed have been an impossible mental chore to change any of those deeply ingrained perceptions.

To those who thrived on sensationalism, it had to have its disappointments. They weren't getting the answers that rhymed with their anti-war jingles and popular songs. In digging for dirt, When it was found out that I didn't kill anybody, avail myself of the charms of the female population of Vietnam, or experiment with drugs, questioners seemed to lose interest, and look for someone who would tell them the things that they wanted to hear. It was as though I was being blamed for missing some of the more destructive consequences of the war, and that I had no idea of what I was talking about. (I was just there, what did I know?) It became quite evident, to me, because I didn't support their cherished perceptions that my views were dismissed as worthless. It's in this spirit that I continue my narrative.

    Xuan Loc was, indeed, a most colorful place, and much more like what Vietnam was like than at Cu Chi. We were in contact with a class of Vietnamese who weren't as concerned about trying to be westernized. They were much less pretentious.

Throughout the whole tour, all of us were given the opportunity to observe Vietnamese in several different settings. We were

A Contradiction of Terms: A 25th Division Analyst's Tour in Vietnam

offered an education that put the whole experience in perspective-if we were receptive to the opportunities. The type and level of our involvement severely limited using what we were being shown by the Vietnamese about what they really wanted and needed. One way of dealing with us was by their imitation of us. Although it's flattering to be thought of in such a manner, it becomes evident it's just a means of getting along. It didn't necessarily mean that they were happy that we were there. They possibly were saying, more or less what they thought we wanted to hear. It was a survival mechanism of the same type that they used when the VC were in control.

The ones who were sincere, and didn't overtly subscribe to this, were the ones that I was most impressed with. They were the ones that I really felt for. It was painful to think about what this place was going to be like, in several years, when this was supposed to be over. My concern was that the people who really trusted us and wanted our help won't only be let down but punished or possibly killed for their association with us. Ultimately, I wanted to know them as they really were, and how they really lived and perceived the future. These people in the Xuan Loc area, I feel came closest to that.

In this place, the pace was much slower and it offered a chance to meet Vietnamese in a whole different setting. I saw that all the tensions of war were there, but in a different form. Considering that men from all different places, were running around their country, for whatever nationalistic reasons, making themselves at home; I think they took it rather well.

I felt as much at home here as I did anywhere in the whole tour. I never stopped missing home, my wife and my family; but a familiarity with the area, and especially with these people, had personalized this situation for me. It made a dramatic difference in my attitude about being here. The ladies who kept the area in order and the other Vietnamese people, who kept the mess hall, were familiar faces. Some of the people on the MACV compound I knew personally, though not by name. In the absence of my contacts to the outside world, this was my reality. Without up-to-date magazines, newspapers and pizza to go, this was my home by circumstance, not by choice. After a few months here, I came to accept it.

In this setting, I felt more at one with the situation here. Rather than going through my tour on a large base camp- where the war can be effectively depersonalized, this situation brought us closer to the people here who had infinitely greater stakes here than the goal of surviving a single year. If they lost, they stood to lose everything. In realizing that there were people out there who really trusted us to help them, it is still difficult, to this day, to rationalize that our intent to assist them was completely fulfilled. One of the greatest tragedies of overall situation was that the governments that carried on the war, on every side, had their own ideas about what the people really wanted and needed, and had little or no feeling as to what was necessary.

ALERT

In order to set the stage for this next episode, the internal political situation within the S2 must be addressed. One way of describing it's that it was frequently complained of, as are all things that are not in one's control; and consequently, difficult if not impossible to act upon. Actually, no one outside of their section interacted with anyone else, unless it was absolutely necessary. Under the pretense of security, this farce was continually perpetuated. Not even within the MID itself was this attitude dispensed with.

This was, in all probability, used as a means of keeping order, within the ranks, and of etching out the limited amount of elbowroom available. Relations were for the most part tolerable; but when push came to shove, some bizarre policies were implemented- even if only for the sake of showing that a given individual was in control, or that a certain individual wished to challenge it. Mind games were routinely used on each other.

Such was the situation between the MIC headquarters, contingent and the counterintelligence section. The nature of their assignments dictated that they be in contact with individuals who wouldn't normally be on the compound. What would be generated from them, theoretically, would be reports of VC/NVA activities, in the area. There was, naturally, a lot of latitude extended to the individuals involved here; and their absence from the compound was generally taken for granted. Whatever was generated; however, wasn't given to OB, probably under the pretense of security- at least as far in my level with the S2 was concerned. Considering the nature of my regular assignments, which ultimately was a sophisticated form of busy work, it would have been nice to know if I were stepping on some toes, by reporting on some things that I had pieced together. Perhaps my ignorance of things, as they were, provided an effective screen for the personalities involved, on both sides of the equation. Even in venturing this, I may still be giving myself more credit than is necessary.

By this time, I was really beginning to understand that our involvement here wasn't something that was going to be readily solved, as had been advertised by the Nixon administration, or the peace groups. I had a sense of this long before, but it was much more pronounced by this time. The situation here was a microcosm of the overall situation that all of us bought into.

A case in point, concerning the 25th MIC at Xuan Loc Forward typifies the situation. Henry was a member of the CI section, who seemed to live in a world of his own. I grant that all of us had our own perceptions of reality; but it was quite evident he wasn't here- when he was here. It was rumored that he was involved with a Vietnamese woman, off post. I'm not too sure why this rumor got so much mileage for it was a situation that to me seemed quite plausible. Those things did happen. I guess they must have been upset that it wasn't happening to them. (Being away from home, I was always upset that it wasn't happening to me. My focus involved getting back and making up for lost time!)

By appearance, Henry was very ordinary looking- too ordinary looking- again the CI mystique. For one reason or another, he just seems to have gotten lucky. Circumstances being what they were, it wasn't such a strange situation, but if this was in the line of duty, he was as compromised as anyone could possibly be. That section being what it was, it was believable The only real problem with that is that he spent a lot of time here, not being here; it was only casually questioned. For a long time, I just heard about him; I wasn't sure that he existed. For most of the time that I knew about him, he was just here on paper.

Eventually, out first sergeant took offense to Henry's absences, and placed him on the duty rosters, which included bunker guard. This was bound to wreak havoc with his schedule; and it quickly did, for the night in question, Henry didn't show up. I know, because I was on the roster after him, next for the duty. Due to Top's intent that Henry show up, I told everyone concerned where I was going to be, in order to cover myself. I was going over to the nearby MACV compound, and enjoy a steak dinner, which, I still feel, to this day that I earned. I didn't know it at the time; but I was about to earn it several times over. It was a nice dinner. My escape from the mess hall made the food very much worth the trip. This was also my first time off the compound, since I arrived in Xuan Loc, in early November. It was quite pleasant. All too soon; however, it was time to return, and resume the normal routine.

I returned to the compound with David Niemeyer and Will Guhman. As I entered, it seemed strangely quiet. Something was very wrong. There were more MP's at the gate than I thought that we had around here. The bunker guard posts were at least doubled. Something bad had happened. Finding out nothing at the gate, except what I had seen, we went to our detachment area, and found the rest of the guys huddled in the hootch. I was told that I was supposed to be on the bunker guard list, and that I should get over there, immediately. Henry never showed up at all, and it was my turn. Something had happened to them, causing their respective manners to change, quite significantly. Larry Moog's satirical views were silent. Richardson's Hemingway-like bravado couldn't be detected. Will Guhman's impressions were silent; and, David

Niemeyer, who was usually never at a loss for words, was. We were on alert, and everyone was scared. This was for real.

I reported to the NCOIC, and he told me of the situation. Just after supper, the Husky compound, just north of here, had been hit with mortar fire. Twelve people were killed, eight Vietnamese and four Americans. A declassified intelligence summary, found in National Archives, indicated that sixteen personnel were wounded including twelve Vietnamese. The mortar apparently hit on or near the mess hall and the basketball court. In the mess hall, some of the Vietnamese day workers were cleaning up, and the GI's were playing basketball. There was no warning. All units in the area were put on alert. This compound was less than a mile from our compound.

I was assigned to a bunker facing the main road, about fifty yards to the left of the main gate. It was here that I spent one of the longest nights that I was ever to spend in Vietnam.

The guys who were in this bunker were for the most part, as opposed to other times, all business. They were, however, quite free with their thoughts. I was glad for that because I wasn't sure what would happen, if someone got too spooked. The reality of the situation dictated that we remember everything that we learned and heard about, and had seen for ourselves. Every lesson, drill, war movie and book, pertaining to situations like this came to mind but the reality of the situation clearly sobered all of us for it.

My thoughts centered on several recollections, that had to do with experiences in high school, and they were most vivid in my mind.

I recalled a reading assignment in high school, set in the Korean War, and titled <u>The Bridges at Toko Ri</u>, by James Michener.

One of the scenes, toward the end of the book, depicted two of the main characters, pinned down by snipers, waiting and hoping for help. One of these character's thoughts were of home, in a country that had next to no idea that there was a war on. I could relate to that.

I remembered, also, a high school assembly, in which an old naval officer told of his experiences in the Second World War. He recalled the times when he thought that he would never see his country again. He vividly described the day of his return; when, he first caught sight of the Golden Gate Bridge, and of the overwhelming feelings of being home. He felt that this was reward enough for defending his country.

I was going through a whole set of emotions, myself, which involved my wondering if this was to be my last night on earth, how and if I'd be remembered, and if my being here had made a difference. In view of the nature of this particular war, I wondered if it would affect, in a grand or miniscule manner, the outcome of the situation. I also mentally prayed, like I never did before. Having gone through all of this, my panic dissipated. I wasn't scared, anymore. I felt those guys, back in the hootch, were having a rougher time coping than I was; because, I was out here doing something. I felt that I had to be here. I'm not sure how I'd have fared, cooped up in that hootch. My associates had inadvertently done me a favor.

Most of the night was spent looking out over the open field, toward Xuan Loc City, wondering what was going to happen next. There were many hopes and prayers, here that something wouldn't happen. A major realization was that, events were out of our hands. Consequently, a lot of prayers, on that particular night went out from that little piece of Vietnam; and, especially from that bunker.

On other bunker guard details, time spent with other members of the detail, in the course of the night, were quite easy-going and informative. In this case, the talk, when it did occur, seemed much more significant; for, it centered around what we were going to do <u>when</u> we got home- not if. An appreciation for the things that weren't available here, as a circumstance of the war, was another major topic of conversation. Although none of us really verbalized it, we were all still scared, and hoped that this night would end.

Even the NCOIC and the rest of the guys, stationed in back of us, behind the sandbags, and others, who were usually looked on in the manner of adversaries, were quiet, reasonable and quite easy to get along with. Probably one reason for this was that all of us, on this night, wanted as much company as possible. I'm sure that the feeling was shared by all.

I want to reintegrate that my comments, on the demeanor of the rest of my unit, were not condemnations of their behavior. I was pretty scared, myself. I don't think, however, that I'd have traded places with any of them, that night. I had to be there, not for the sake of the detail, but for my own experience. Where Henry was that night and whatever happened to him, ultimately, I'm not sure, but it was of little consequence that night. As the night wore on, we all got to know what each of us was all about. I felt that this was much more profound than many of the bull sessions that I was privy to or within earshot of, in my own unit. I don't recall any of their names, and probably wouldn't recognize any of them on sight; but we shared some very important lessons on the absurdity of war, and the reality that we're all in this together, even now.

Eventually, morning did come, and we were all still there. For about the next week or so, a modified alert remained in effect. My detachment, on the next night, was out on the perimeter, near our area, for part of the night. The most noise, during that evening was a helicopter, equipped with a loud speaker. It circled around, playing Christmas carols. It was rather distracting in this context; but I guess it was the thought that counted.

At home there was a postal strike going on. Though I didn't know it the time, news of the mortar attack at Xuan Loc had reached home, but there was no way to let my family know that I was unhurt, and that the attack was on the adjacent compound. Eventually, I did manage to get a MARS call out, which was reassuring to both my family and me.

A Christmas in Vietnam

As Christmas time was drawing near, the situation gradually normalized. It was difficult, however, to get into the spirit of the season. With temperatures in the 90's, and not chance for a White Christmas, we had to make it with what we had. Somehow, an artificial tree was obtained, and decorated with what we had on hand. A Christmas party was planned and organized. It was decided that the party would be held on Christmas Eve- all day. On a much higher level there was a Christmas truce in the works, which resulted in a very special Christmas present.

The truce gave us the opportunity to take a day off from the war. For our unit, we were also given a choice between two outings. We could either go to the Bob Hope show, in Long Binh, or spend the day in Saigon. I felt I had to weigh the decision carefully- this was for posterity! It was quite a difficult choice. I wanted, obviously, to do both, which, at the time, was quite impossible. It came down to choosing the thing that I might not have a chance to do again, under the present circumstances. I opted for the trip to Saigon; which, I felt, after this war was all over, might never be the same. Bob Hope, I reasoned, I might be able to see, back in the states, when he was in the general area. With our individual decisions made, plans were made for Christmas day.

Shortly, before Christmas day, we received our highest ranking and most distinguished visitor, the CINCUSARPAC commander,

A Contradiction of Terms: A 25th Division Analyst's Tour in Vietnam

Admiral John S. McCain. Admiral McCain was Commander of all the U.S. Forces, in the Pacific. This included also, the U.S. Forces in Vietnam. He arrived when we were working in the in the Order of Battle shop. When he arrived, we all stood at attention, until told to stand at ease. Admiral McCain was a short, white-haired man, about as tall as my grandfather was. I was later told that he was a submariner, during the Second World War. In my turn, he spoke to me, asking where I was from, and how I was doing. He was very personable and seemed genuinely interested in my responses. He spoke briefly, to everyone. He told us how important it was for us to do what we were doing, and how our efforts must be brought to a successful conclusion. This could have been the standard line of a high-level military commander, something Patton-like; but there was more to it than that. I learned, much later, that he had more than enough reason for wanting this war to end. His son was a prisoner in North Vietnam. Unlike most high-level American military men and politicians of the era, he carried an added burden of uncertainty about his son's fate. Outwardly, he didn't show this, but his being there said much more than words ever could. He could have been home at Christmas, with the rest of his family, but he chose to be here with us. This was possibly his way of being close to his son. I wasn't aware of his personal situation, to grasp the significance of this at the time. In retrospect, it was one of the most touching experiences of the war for me. (I did get to meet Senator John McCain, in September, 20015. I got to tell him about his father spending that part of Christmas with us,)

Photos in my possession show how we celebrated Christmas at Xuan Loc Forward. The Christmas party that we had was the one of the few times that we were all together as a unit. It was reminiscent of old times- eight months before, when I first arrived. We started a charcoal fire, got some steaks from the mess hall, before they could do anything to them. Someone bought French bread from one of the markets in Xuan Loc. We got some ice to chill the beer and sodas, in an open, U-Haul trailer, used as makeshift cooler. Butter was melted for the French bread, which wasn't a difficult chore, considering that it was already about 95 degrees- even before approaching the grill. AFVN was playing some of the old songs and some of the well-known public service announcements that had to do with protecting yourself against malaria and various social diseases, not necessarily in any order, and getting ready for DEROS- the preferred way out of here. The way that we celebrated any holiday was sort of a time-honored tradition, if not a ritual for all breaks in the work routine. It was what we could put together, in a given time and place, with what we had. Everyone had a good time. The atmosphere was very relaxed. Were it up to me, I'd have done this weekly. Actually- some of us probably did, it just wasn't publicized. Larry Moog, in particular, made it his personal duty to maintain a country club atmosphere.

Mass was said on Christmas day, in the chapel, by the Catholic chaplain, who appeared here several times a week.

To get to Saigon, we had to get an early start. It took about an hour to get there. On the way, taking Route 1, we stopped at Camp Frenzel Jones to and pick up two personnel from Xuan Loc Forward. One was a Frenchman from the interrogation section, whom I had known at Cu Chi, and another that I don't think that I met before. It was claimed that the Frenchman knew his way around Saigon; and I had no reason to disbelieve him. As we passed Long Binh, proper, we saw the stands where Bob Hope's show was being set up. I had some misgivings about the choice but decided on Saigon.

On the outskirts of Long Binh, Vietnamese could be seen selling all sorts of things, out of simple booths, making a living

A Contradiction of Terms: A 25th Division Analyst's Tour in Vietnam

as best they could around Long Binh. With so many Americans around, it had to be better for them, than some other areas, for a steady income. Along the road, conditions were much worse. It was a very different way of living. I felt that these people really wanted for very little, except a place to live, a little food and to be left alone. Circumstances from within and without their country made it next to impossible.

Cholon is located on the eastern outskirts of Saigon itself. As we rode further into this district, there were more and more houses, and people, proportionate to the proximity to the city. There were more people around here than I had ever seen in my life. There were people on foot, combined with bicycles, Jeeps, buses, motorcycles, and Lambretta trucks. They were all around, and in front and behind us, as far as the eye could see. I was told that this area had a population density comparable to that of Hong Kong. It was quite a colorful and exciting experience. If I ever felt like a tourist, in a far-off country, I had that feeling then. Before this, I saw relatively few Vietnamese. I usually only met them, if they came on the compound. Now I was in their world; and, it was really exciting. I'm not sure if it was because this was a day of truce, or that travel through here could be accomplished any time, but I completely enjoyed this chance to get out; I wouldn't have minded doing it out again.

As we crossed a bridge over the Saigon River, we saw some of the port facilities that received a lot of supplies for our side. (and probably the other side too) It was comparable to some of the storage areas at the Port of Baltimore. It was a huge and quite elaborate port facility. There were incredible stores of supplies sitting on the docks for processing. It was such a contrast to the sights that I had been familiar with, in the rural areas, and by the roadside. In the more remote areas, the situation would have been even more pronounced, than my personal observations. These discoveries made me even more curious about this country full of paradoxes, some of which, I was just beginning to realize Americans had created themselves. I had only got to see a relatively small part of it.

Saigon itself was much more commercialized and swarming with all kinds of people and vehicular traffic. Some of the things that made it different from Cholon were the government buildings and the American embassy, and other formidable brick and stone buildings. The University of Saigon was pointed out to me, and I promptly snapped a picture of it. Because of bad batteries in my new camera, I only got two pictures of Saigon. I'd have wanted to go back for more. Unfortunately, this wasn't to happen. Of any landmarks that were pointed out, I doubt that I'd have found them on my own. These days, it's probably unrecognizable.

We parked across the street from the USO, in Saigon. It was a rather nondescript building, and just one structure of a block full of large row-type brick buildings. It was only recognizable by the sign. When we parked, a little Vietnamese boy approached us; and it was bargained with him that he would watch our jeep, and that he would get some money, if he watched it properly, meaning that if it was still there, when we got back.

Some of the others wanted to see the rest of Saigon. I was mainly interested in enjoying the hospitality of the USO. A nice turkey dinner was being offered, and I got my name on a list to call home. I really enjoyed the whole experience of the USOs hospitality.

The arrangement of the USO facility was quite interesting. In the back of the building was a courtyard where. When you looked up, it appeared that the space was blasted, rather than modeled out of this crowded area of buildings. The yard was arranged nicely; but the upper stories of the adjacent structures looked like they had taken quite a beating. Neighboring Vietnamese could be seen looking down on us, also enjoying the sights and sounds.

The USO people were very friendly. I was fed quite well, all day. I watched part of a football game on television, and later wandered around the area. Later on, I ventured outside, several times. On two of these occasions, I got some general ideas of what this city was really like, for better or worse. In the course of this day, I received quite an education on this particular area. It was one of many things to see in the course of this day.

The first time that I stepped out, the result almost encouraged me to stay in. There was the sound of automatic rifle fire. I don't know why I ventured out, knowing what it was, but I did. Across the street, and to my right, there were some South Vietnamese soldiers firing M16s into the air. Maybe it was their way of celebrating Christmas. I wasn't sure. Someone, probably the National Police, stopped them, almost immediately. With so many people around, it seemed a rather dangerous thing to do; I guess that they had seen worse, done worse, and were used to it.

The next time out, I decided that I wanted to take a couple of pictures, with my new Polaroid camera. I didn't have to wait very long to pick a subject- he picked me. A National policeman motioned for me to take a picture of him and I was quick to oblige such an eager subject. While I was setting the camera, and having him pose, I noticed that I was gathering a crowd. I wasn't sure what was going on. I wasn't about to believe that they had never seen a camera before. I snapped a picture and waited for it to develop. I didn't know at the time that the batteries that powered the light meter were dead. As I waited, the crowd also waited in eager anticipation- I'm still not sure why, for the photo to develop. They seemed a lot more excited than I was. When the minute elapsed, I peeled the paper off of a black print- and the crowd moaned along with me. I adjusted the light, and had the policeman stand back again. I took another picture- and it still wasn't working. I made my apologies to everyone, smiled- and they all smiled, yelled back, and waved, as I retreated back into the USO. To this day, I still can't figure out what I was doing that drew the crowd; but I think that if I ever take up acting or stand-up comedy, I'd like to have a crowd like that as my audience.

When I returned to the USO, I had the Christmas dinner, and watched some more of the football game. My number finally came up to call my wife and family. It was great to hear their voices, and not have to say "over" as with the MARS calls. I was happy for the opportunity to call home. At that time, a three-minute call from Saigon to Baltimore cost about twenty-five dollars. I can't imagine what such a call would cost now. I believe that some organization connected with the USO had paid for a lot of the calls. I sure that I speak for a lot of guys, who were over here, when I say to whoever was responsible for this should know that it was very much appreciated.

At the end of the day, we met at the jeep, which was still there, and started our trip back to Xuan Loc .The ride was fairly uneventful. The scenery was pretty; I saw several other areas that I hadn't seen before. We came back to Long Binh, and parted company with the guys from the other detachment. We saw the stands and the stage, where Bob Hope had appeared. I promised myself, that if given the opportunity, I'd see one of his shows. [I did get that chance in 1976 and 1979 when he was in Baltimore, for the Preakness Festivals.]

What I remember the most about the trip back was how beautiful and colorful this country was. I couldn't help thinking how much more beautiful it would be if there weren't a war going on. We got a sample of it that day. None of us were armed; and, as far as I'm concerned, it was a great feeling. I was all for a much more permanent arrangement, for all the parties involved. This day was yet another instance in which I met a different group of Vietnamese people, probably the largest that could ever be encountered; and I was impressed with their friendliness. I had been told many stories of how you had to watch out, in places like that. That wasn't my experience. I wanted to go again; but one thing or another prevented that from happening. I hope to return some day. I was well aware that circumstances were much more serious than I had encountered, but my personal contact with them was positive.

WINTER IN XUAN LOC

The Christmas celebration ended shortly after the New Year's Eve party and normal routine was resumed with the survivors of the festivities, who were left standing. Security seemed to be of little consequence. It was hoped that the other side was taking a holiday too. They probably did, for nothing happened. On New Year's Eve, I stopped much earlier than others did; but not before David Niemeyer introduced me to Liebfraumilch.

The routine of the S2/OB resumed with the knowledge that, probably, in several months; the unit would cease operations, and stand down. This was still not likely to happen before my scheduled time to go home. This was comforting, for I didn't want to go to another unit; I wanted to go home earlier, if possible. At any rate, there wouldn't be enough time to go to another unit. In the meantime, here, it was business as usual. Intsums, Parintreps, visitors, and briefing details were all part of the daily work pattern.

My pre-occupations outside of the shop involved writing home, basketball with David Niemeyer and Will Guhman, recording some of the Beatles music that would add to my collection at home, and trying to teach David chess, which seemed, at times, a lost cause. Occasionally, some of us would go over to the MACV compound, for a steak dinner. It was always great to get out for a little while.

A Contradiction of Terms: A 25th Division Analyst's Tour in Vietnam

During January, I pulled the evening shift, coming in late in the afternoon, and closing up the OB shop about midnight. In regard to current events, this was about the time when Alan Shepard landed on the Moon, during the Apollo XIV mission. I spent a lot of the shift writing letters, and listening to the radio, to basketball games and music on AFVN, from Saigon. I also made another tape to send home, along with taping some other tapes that were never sent. They were never really finished, and I sent them back by surface mail-, which arrived about a month, after I returned home.

I didn't really mind the shift at all. It gave me some quiet time, so that I could write, and do all the little things that helped preserve my sanity. One of the things in particular kept me occupied, but it drove others out of their minds was my guitar playing. I tried from time to time to learn how to play it but made only very slow progress. My efforts were not really appreciated. I couldn't understand why. At any rate, I didn't get much encouragement.

The quarters situation was so familiar, it could be determined, once within earshot, just who was home. I had my Beatles music (and my guitar!) and music that I had taped before I left home in April. Mark Richardson seemed to like ballads, and popular music. One of his favorite groups was <u>Bread</u>. Larry Moog had a Judy Collins Album that seemed to be played constantly- until he got hold of the soundtrack of Hair! Larry seemed to spend most of his time there; consequently, before we left, all of us had memorized every word of every song of that Judy Collins Album and the complete soundtrack of Hair. Just when we thought that we couldn't take any more of this, AFVN started playing James Taylor songs, and the soundtrack of *Jesus Christ, Superstar*. <u>Three Dog Night</u> was also gaining in popularity, although they had been around for several years. All this music combined was one of the signs that we had settled into a routine, that all of us subconsciously hoped won't be interrupted until we landed at Travis Air Force Base, in California.

One of my goals, besides getting home alive, involved getting my promotion to E5. My early departure from the RA class, at Fort Holabird, had deprived me of that permanent rank. The extra money would have been very nice. My leaving for Vietnam was compounded by the money problems associated with not achieving that rank. Taking into consideration the meager wages and the $65.00 a month combat pay, it was still more a matter of honor than of economics- although, I don't think that the money wouldn't have corrupted me.

It was an added source of irritation and frustration when the finance section caught up with me, the first pay that I received in country. The result of this was that I had about $15.00 left to spend, during the whole month of May. With as much as I knew about Cu Chi base camp and what to spend money on, it really didn't make that much difference. It did encourage me to stay close to home, not spend money on junk food, and to stick close to the mess hall for sustenance. I'm glad I didn't know then how bad the mess hall really was. It was a fortunate circumstance, that I was ignorant of this, at the time. That month in poverty could have been much worse.

By the time the next pay period came around, I found some of the good places to eat, discovered Vietnamese pizzas, and found the souvenir shop, and the main PX. From that point, my tour settled into a fairly normal routine. In Cu Chi, enlisted rank was never really an issue. In Xuan Loc, it was a different story. As far as I was concerned (or not overtly concerned) it was just a technicality-an accident of the Army. I was a victim of circumstance, and felt that the situation would right itself, given the opportunity to change it. I was young and naive, and never really believed in terrible things, or was aware of them- until I got to Holabird. I thought that bureaucratic foul-ups were the stuff that movies were made out of, but I was brand new to this.

The point of contention was something entirely unexpected; it was something that I really should have seen coming, considering that I was dealing with the military. When we arrived in Xuan Loc, in November, the mess hall situation was such that, the NCOs were served by dining room assistants-Vietnamese girls, who helped out in the kitchen. The food left a lot to be desired, but the service was good. I'd, at first, go with the rest of the group, for lunch and dinner. Nobody, including myself really thought too much of it. I was the only E4, in the Xuan Loc forward MID, and really didn't wish to be singled out.

Headquarters detachment seemed really intimidated by the MID personnel. I could tell that, because the first sergeant would salute me when I was in his proximity. Apparently, because I didn't wear rank insignia- and neither did the other detachment personnel (until this incident) he thought I was an officer. Maybe he didn't like that. (I'm sure he didn't like that!) Once we were made to wear the rank insignia the situation changed for the worse. From this point on, I couldn't eat in the mess hall with the same people that I worked with. It was quite a difficult thing to accept. The solution seemed fairly simple. When I heard that the promotion board for E5 would be convened in the near future, I made every preparation to be ready for my time in front of that board. Until then, I had to eat in the lower enlisted mess. It was the same food, but I got to see how bad it really was. I missed the familiar company, when I had to eat there, and sometimes would partake of the food stores of PX food and the C-rations, that we kept in the barracks area. I only ate in the mess hall, when I had to. It wasn't as though these guys were my ideal dinner companions- but they were literally all I had. I actually came to miss them at mealtimes. I felt that I was singled out, and really started to resent it. I'm not quite sure what my associates thought about it, but it wasn't much that they could do about it, either.

I used this as another motivating factor that kindled my fervor to make rank as soon as possible. To this end, I prepared, as best

I could; being drilled with questions on things that would be likely to be asked at the promotion board proceeding. I tried to examine every source that I thought would help. I asked around about what was expected, and prepared as best I could. I'd give it my best shot.

In consideration of the upcoming promotion board interview, Lt. Mitchum put me on the roster with the E5s, to participate in the daily briefings with the 2nd Brigade commander, Colonel Ulatowski, representing the order of battle section, of the S2. I had to indicate the points that were referred to, by the briefer, as he went down his list of contacts for that period. It was fairly menial detail, but I felt a part of it and I was glad to be there. It was just nice to do something different. I appreciated the opportunity to participate there.

In early February, the promotion board convened, and I took my turn to make my appearance. It was held in Long Binh, so we got an early morning start from Xuan Loc. On the way, we stopped at Frenzel Jones to pick up somebody else for their board appearance.

When I was interviewed, I was asked all types of questions, and I felt that I answered them in a reasonably intelligent manner. I remember best, questions prompting me to describe my duties as an intelligence analyst, in the order of battle shop. I gave them answers as to general function, and some examples of its application to 2/25th operations. I wasn't sure of where to stop, in talking about operations, so I picked some examples that didn't, as far as I knew, deal with anything that was current. I had misgivings about in discussing even that, for the general rule wasn't to discuss <u>anything</u> out of the shop, especially, within earshot of any Vietnamese, no matter how much they had been cleared. The premise was that all of them probably knew every VC or were relatives to one in their particular area, far better than any of us ever could. It might have been nice to check our information against theirs, but that was another department, and they usually weren't talking.

I wasn't too sure what these officers had absorbed, I hoped that my evaluation would be considered by my general knowledge and familiarization with the job.

When the interview was completed, we had lunch at the Chinese restaurant, at Long Binh. The building itself was of incredible size, larger than any building, on our compound in Xuan Loc, or in Xuan Loc City, itself. The food and the service were really nice. I enjoyed a meal of some sort of highly seasoned shrimp and was happy to be temporary reunited with some of my Xuan Loc associates at dinner. At any rate it was always nice to get out.

The manner of the Xuan Loc rear personnel was somewhat puzzling. I knew that the guy who had more time than me came with us, and quite possibly, there was some factionalism involved, but when I first met these people, I was looked at and talked to like I had been through a major trauma. It reminded me of a time that I observed an individual who had just come in from the field, on to our compound- and he looked the part. He gave me the impression, just by his appearance, that these are the people who really caught the worst of it, and that Xuan Loc Forward was looked on by them as a rear area, by comparison. My questioning of this character verified what I had thought. I was in awe. To my surprise, that was the way the Frenzel Jones people were questioning me. This was in view of the alert, and the action around what had happened in December. I'm not sure that they heard and under what circumstances, or if it was a buildup from someone else, prior to my appearance here, but I had this feeling from the reception that I had arrived from some outpost. In relation to Xuan Loc rear, I actually did come from an outpost, but I really didn't feel any different for that experience. They probably had a better look at what we were up against, on a larger scale; that may have been a major factor, in their interaction with me.

Several weeks later, I found out that I didn't get the promotion. I was reminded that this wasn't a reflection on my job performance, but the availability of only one slot, and that only my time in grade was probably the deciding factor. I was still rather depressed and angry, for a time. I had to write home to relay the bad news. The board's assessment of me did prompt a letter from Major Moore to be put in my file, in regard to my performance. He recommended me highly, for promotion. It was a glowing recommendation. Until then, I had no idea how they felt about my contributions to the detachment, if it was thought about, at all. Lt. Mitchum mouthed, basically, what Major Moore had written. He also acknowledged my disappointment about the board results- a sort of 'keep the faith' admonition. I appreciated his taking the time to say that.

SIDE TRIPS

One of the few voluntary details here involved riding into Long Binh, with the company clerk, early in the morning. This being a preferred detail, I got to go only once in a while. One of the ulterior motives in undertaking this detail was to get off of the compound for a while and out of the daily routine. Although we had to get up early in the morning, once on the way, it was, normally, a pleasant routine with a few notable exceptions.

Technically, the passenger on this detail was riding shotgun and had to constantly be on the lookout, especially while going through some of the areas of recent VC/NVA activity. Trang Baum, Trang Bang, Hung Loc and Hung Nia were major market areas, that looked quite normal; but we were quite aware that the other side had to use these areas quite extensively, also.

In Trang Baum, there was a Texaco station that normally caught my eye and reminded me of the advertising phrase that they used for so many years. I wasn't quite so sure, in this case if you really wanted to trust your car, or anything else, to the man who wears the star. In these parts, a big red star meant something else entirely.

These trips were, for the most part, uneventful. On one of the early morning trips, we were involved in some sort of rolling back up on Route One. There was a convoy, on the road and that

limited zipping along as we were used to. At one of the places that we stopped, just outside of Xuan Loc, there was a man standing near the side of the road- with a rifle. I wanted to take for granted that he was part of the Regional/Provincial Force, sort of like a South Vietnamese State Militia or Highway Patrol. I commented to Snyder about the
'Ruff-Puffs' and pointed out the guy. I asked him if he could tell where he was from, and he said that he didn't know. At this answer, I decided that I'd only get upset if he and the driver did. I felt he was starting to get upset. The traffic started up, in a minute, and we left the area, without incident.

On another occasion I got to see a side of the ARVNs that I wasn't completely aware of. A few days, before, we were treated to a surprise, of sorts. The 18th ARVN Division, on which we had depended on, for security, located adjacent to our compound had, vanished without warning. No explanation was given; we just woke up one morning, and they were gone. As a consequence, we had to compensate, by using some of our own units from the field for the defense of the compound. This incident didn't do anything to reinforce our feelings of security in that particular area, and our liking for the 18th ARVN. Several days later, I was on the morning run to Frenzel-Jones, when we encountered an ARVN convoy, heading east, on Route One. My previous encounters with South Vietnamese soldiers had been friendly. If I wasn't liked, it was never shown, and I was at least tolerated. My usual banter with Sergeant Kahn was what I was used to. Up to that time, with few exceptions, I never really met an ARVN that I didn't like. I had this idea that we were all on the same side, and was usually at ease, when a conversation occurred with one of them.

On my trips, along Route One, I usually waved, and flashed a peace sign, to whoever looked friendly. It broke any tensions, on my part and I liked to think that I made a friend along the way.

A Contradiction of Terms: A 25th Division Analyst's Tour in Vietnam

In this particular instance, as we passed the convoy, I caught sight of an ARVN soldier, with some others, in battle gear, riding on top of a personnel carrier. I flashed a smile and a peace sign at him. In return he gave me the finger and started shouting at me. He continued for what seemed like a very long time to make threatening gestures. Words wouldn't normally get my attention, but what he was doing with his M16 was really beginning to concern me. Time seems to do strange things in this type of circumstance. I tried not to appear upset, though I was really stunned by his reaction. This soldier was so upset, that he was upsetting everybody else around him- quite possibly because I was holding an M16 too, and they weren't sure of what I was going to do, either. They had to physically sit him down and try to calm him. I asked Larry what was going on. I still wasn't sure what had happened. He explained that they were on their way to operations in Cambodia. I, then, didn't have to know any Vietnamese to understand what this ARVN was saying, now. As far as he was concerned, this was our war, not theirs; he was angry and frustrated that he was going where he thought Americans should be going. He knew we would be leaving them with the war all too soon. I understood him. He was saying what a lot of others were too afraid to say. He was scared and frustrated. I knew the feeling, all too well. It was a feeling that would return to me periodically to remind me how much I really hated it here. The way that I personally tried to handle it was to take one day at a time, and then start another. I felt for him and all the other South Vietnamese, who would bear the responsibility for maintaining their country, when we left. Like it was supposed to happen in the first place, it would eventually all depend on them. They had every right to be scared.

On other trips to Long Binh, there were other opportunities to just enjoy the scenery, and appreciate what a beautiful country, Vietnam really was. The whole range of a long and interesting history was evident, although I was aware of only the rudiments of it. A lot of it was supplemented by these trips on Route One. The market places of Trang Bang, Hung Loc, Hung Nia, and Xuan Loc City, itself gave me the impression that, with some variations, like the Texaco pumps, the bicycles and the motorized vehicles, the market place may have looked the same a hundred years ago.

I got to look again at the two main churches between The Hung Loc/Hung Nia area and Xuan Loc City- Buddhist temple and a Catholic Church. Both of them reflected the major religious trends in Indochina, within the last two centuries. The Buddhist temple looked as though it had been there for centuries; the Catholic Church was fairly modern. It was probably constructed in the 1950's [Cite description in <u>55 Days: The Fall of South Vietnam</u>, by Alan Dawson, Englewood: Prentis-Hall, Inc., 1977.]

    The types of housing ranged from thatched huts, located near Long Binh to the box-like, stuccoed structures of Xuan Loc City. The beautiful French mansion, that I first noticed around Christmastime, located somewhere between Trang Bang and Banana Mountain, always fascinated me. Its presence spoke of the time when the French were a major influence in Indochina. This was just a hint of what it was like in Saigon, in years past.

    The agricultural, rural Vietnam, as opposed to the urban, Hong Kong-like sprawl of the Saigon area could be observed, in composite, on these trips. The Vietnamese people, themselves, were fascinating to observe. People on foot, with water buffaloes, bicycles, motorbikes, and Lambretta trucks could be seen, along the road, in any given place, between Long Binh and Xuan Loc .In the rural market areas, the local Vietnamese sported their water buffaloes; while motorized transportation use seemed to be heavier, in proportion to the proximity of the big military bases, airports and of Saigon, itself. There were many times, when we were traveling along the road, at a speed we considered pretty fast, when a busload of Vietnamese would zip right past us.

Every time that I got to see this part of the country, and the people, I hoped that someday that I could see this country without the war, and the people could be seen as they really were. I wouldn't hesitate to return to see that.

REALIZATIONS

Even though technically a soldier in the field, I never personally harbored negative feelings for the other side. Actually, I feel that in doing this particular job right, an understanding of why they were out there in the first place and what they were doing was essential. I constantly harbored an idealistic hope that things could somehow be worked out for everyone involved- including myself, so that I could go home in one piece. I never really saw myself as one of Sergeant Rock's Howling Commandos, anyway. My views, it seems, as I got closer to the war, tended to be less war-like. After I had met some of these people, face to face, even though in a position of advantage, I got to see how absurd wars really were.

The reality of the situation was that, even with all the assistance that we had rendered to the GVN- (a lot of it misguided), we seemed to have continuously missed the mark. I'm not quite sure the South Vietnamese knew what they wanted- except to survive. The achievement of the stated objective, which was to assist the South Vietnamese, had been completely obscured by conflicting political considerations, on many levels. I wasn't completely aware of it, then. We may have been over here, thinking that we were fulfilling that purpose, but on the highest levels, what was said, and what was done, many times, were two different things. The tragedy was that, at critical times (like when your life is on the line) what we were told, and was really happening were two different matters. What the media wrote further served to confuse the situation; they were correct, however in causing people to wonder what was really happening here, but fell far short of any really constructive criticism.

There were Americans who did the best they could to do their jobs and found that their own people were countering them. The raid of the prison camp, at Son Tay, in North Vietnam, in early 1971 was one of the most graphic examples of this phenomenon. Analysts had information that American POWs were in this area at a given time. The information was sat on and by the time the raid was executed, the Americans had long-since been removed. It was quite an impressive operation, and it held out great hope that it could be carried out. It was more of a show than anything else. Along with the information that would make the operation feasible, it also had to be known that American POWs with the exception of being in the Hanoi Hilton were never kept in the same place for very long. Information, therefore, that there were Americans in a given area had to be acted on immediately. Apparently, it wasn't a high-level priority.

In all fairness, however, I've read, from other sources that the North Vietnamese had standing orders to kill POWs if an attempt to free them was imminent. These orders were carried out most consistently, for in almost forty documented attempts, only one man was rescued, but died of his wounds.

It was evident, by this time that whenever we left, The South Vietnamese would be truly by themselves and on their own. The time was drawing near for our involvement here to be winding down, and ready or not, we were leaving. If this stated objective of assisting the South Vietnamese was to work, it had to be taken up then, by the people of Vietnam. The choice was theirs. For their sakes, I hoped that they would be ready. From my position, all I could do for them was to hope. What they really needed couldn't be given in the form of material assistance. Our leaving, too early or too late, wasn't going to affect the outcome; it was how the burden was to be assumed. South Vietnamese ploys to make us stay were counter-productive to the stated intent of assistance to them. It rings too much of cliché to continually say that the situation here was too complex to deal with. The reality was that it was always in the hands of the People of Vietnam. For thousands of years, they had fought many foes, including themselves, to establish and maintain their identity as Indochinese. They never needed to be taught how to fight. All we seemed to accomplish was to show them other ways, to do that. The same could be said of being free. I hope in the long run that we may have had a hand in reminding them of that, and of achieving it. In the years to come, when all wounds are healed, on both sides, and all the rhetoric has died down, my prediction is that it will be seen that we really did want to help; we just didn't know how.

HOI CHAN

I had the rare opportunity of talking to an NVA lieutenant, who had defected, and was being debriefed. It gave me a valuable opportunity to get a look at the other side of the equation. It was quite an interesting session. This incident really caused me to wonder what wars were really all about.

One of the programs utilized by the American and South Vietnamese governments to bring NVA and VC over to our side was called the Chieu Hoi or "Open Arms" program. Medical attention, food, money and land were offered as inducements to the NVA/VC to leave their respective units, and come in from the field. One of the obvious benefits of this (when it worked for us) was the intelligence information that could be gained from someone who had reasonable knowledge of a particular unit or units. Information about who they were and how many were in their unit, their location and function helped in evaluating the enemy situation in the area. Some of the defectors were very knowledgeable; others had little to offer.

One of the disadvantages of this program was that the NVA and VC could also use it against us. There were instances in which certain units were starving and demoralized; and this program was at times used as a means to recuperate. There was also the possibility that they could give us false information. There were other instances of some being disenchanted with the program, and what the US/GVN had to offer, and returned to their units. Usually these things took care of themselves. If what they had told us was true, then they couldn't return to their unit without suffering the consequences. If what they said was false, they not only forfeited whatever was offered, but they could also be turned over to the South Vietnamese, the Thais or the Australians, who weren't into such games. It was more preferable to defect to an American unit. It's quite probable that there was a lot of deception and counter-deception in this program. It seems however, that in our holding out the threat of being given over to the ARVNs or any other non-American unit (who routinely took no prisoners) the incidence of this happening was reduced significantly.

During the time that we were involved in this area, one of the things that we were skeptical of was this program for repatriation of North Vietnamese and Viet Cong. From past experience, there were many abuses of this program, and both sides were to blame for this.

The person that I met was brought to the MID, and informally questioned. He was fairly relaxed, and not really nervous about talking with Frank Croty, one of the interrogators and Frank Canoli, from Imagery Interpretation. It was a very open session. As we came in, we were introduced around, and were informally there to answer some of his questions about us. It a rather interesting and backward sort of interrogation, in which he probably learned more about us, and the way that we lived than we did about him. He was a lieutenant in the 274th NVA Regiment, one of the major units involved against us, in the Xuan Loc district. For a variety of reasons, not the least of was lack of food, he apparently decided to take us up on our offer. He talked about his unit, and the other units in the area, that he knew about. Happenings of this sort, when they work out, are an order of battle analyst's dream come true. As an example, one item of significance was that, considering its position, 74th Arty, (74th Artillery Regiment) would put us in deep trouble- if they had artillery. Our compound would have been a major target. The information, when collated with other sources, turned out to be very good. It helped to explain the mortaring of Husky compound, two months before.

In comparing the way that he lived, with ours, we had a great time of it. He couldn't get over, what was to him an incredible amount of food, sodas and beer all around him. He also noticed the informal way we dressed- particularly me. At the time, I was wearing shorts, a sport shirt, and shower shoes, which I got from home. He was laughing at me; I must have looked the part of an American tourist.

He was an NVA officer, about my age, pressed into service, by the standard NVA enlistment program. (They were much more subtle and forceful than American draft boards.) He had, considering the circumstances of being around Americans who he was taught took no prisoners, literally put his life in our hands. How he got here, it wasn't completely clear to me. His decision, however, considering his former resolve, must have been a very difficult one. This particular incident personalized the war for me. It shouldn't have taken a war that somebody else started, to bring us together.

This wasn't, however, the last that I we saw of him. The next day, when we went into Frenzel Jones, on the morning run, we stopped by the hospital, in Long Binh, to visit Terry Eways, a member of the II section, who had a bout with malaria. He seemed to be getting along just fine. We talked for a while and made ourselves at home. As we talked, out of the corner of my eye, I saw another familiar face: It was the Hoi Chanh that we had talked to the night before! He was getting a checkup at the EVAC, probably a preliminary procedure to his processing. We laughed at the coincidence that he was in the same area. He was glad, also, see some familiar faces.

Later, after we left for the hospital, we ate at the Chinese restaurant and had quite a nice meal. We also had an informal sightseeing tour of the Long Binh base camp. Particularly impressive, and totally out of place, was a golf course. I had heard about this, but I thought that it was just an exaggeration. If the North Vietnamese had ever preserved an area representative of the American capacity to waste money and resources, this place should have been the one. This was yet another example that contrasted particular areas of South Vietnam. It was much more than a little too much.

After lunch, we returned to the Xuan Loc compound around the middle of the afternoon, just in time to meet, yet again, the Hoi Chanh, whom we met twice before. He had walked out of the hospital, and the gate of Long Binh base camp, caught a bus, and was back in Xuan Loc, before we returned. Just when I thought that we were going to adopt this character, he was sent on to II Field Force, for further processing. Like a lot of Vietnamese I had met I don't know what happened to him. For my own point of view, he, in his own way made me aware of the absurdity of war. Although I knew him for a very short time, I will never forget him. This was yet another instance which prompts one to think about what this whole thing was all about, and how much I wanted to be home and out of it, where I didn't have to really think about it. It didn't really work that way, however. It was far too late, to not think about it.

XUAN LOC MENANGERIE

Along with settling into a certain area, there is a propensity to also have pets, or some other kind of animal around. My unit was no exception. This place wasn't the first, in which we kept any kind of pets. At 25th MIC, we had a dog named Hank. He was taken to Frenzel Jones, when we moved east. These pets, not so curiously, reflected the personalities of their keepers- sometimes so closely that I wondered if these people hadn't taken some of their survival traits from these animals. The preferred kind, further reflecting their personalities and the situation were the kind that were independent, and generally took care of themselves. For others, lacking other persons to be responsible for, this was also a reasonable preoccupation. The animals that we did keep around also came to be accepted as members of the unit, with their own distinct personalities.

Probably, as with other units, mascots or pets were commonplace. The more exotic or unique the animal was- all the better. On the Xuan Loc compound, we had such an animal, in our unit a dog named, Snarffle. The advance elements of the 25th MID had somehow adopted this dog when he was a very small puppy, parents unknown. In a very few months, he grew in what seemed to be some very strange ways.

I wrote home about him; one letter, in particular was devoted to just a description of him. Snarffle was the star attraction of the detachment, and people would come from all over the compound, just to see what everyone was talking about. He seemed to take the notoriety in stride; and, as much as we could tell, he didn't let it go to his head. He was unpretentious and had a pleasant personality; and his honest reactions to new discoveries were frequently overwhelming. A case in point would be the first time that Snarffle saw a horse. In this area, to me this was a rare occurrence. To him, this large animal must have looked, to him, to be the biggest dog that he had ever seen. At this, he stood by the side of the road, completely absorbed, wondering how he was going to get to know it! A vehicle coming down the road almost hit him, and he didn't even notice it.

Snarffle was a lazy sort of dog; he didn't really like to expend a lot of energy, if he didn't have to. He knew how to relax. It was never difficult to get a picture of him, doing one of the things that he did best. He loved shady spots, and he was an expert in knowing where to find them.

Besides having this talent for relaxation, there was something that he was even more noted for. Pound for pound, he was one of the most avid beer drinkers that I've ever known- the quintessential lap dog! He was probably weaned on beer. He liked drinking, especially with Larry Moog. They were the most creative and prolific beer drinking pair that the MID ever produced. Snarffle also had a taste for vermouth, and Larry would treat him, from time to time. He was a quiet drinker, and never got surly when he drank; his gate would, however, give him away. Although, he would pal around a lot with Larry, he was a pretty independent sort, and, within reason, he went where he pleased. He never really roamed very far, and he always knew when to come home, especially when the shadow was over the yardarm. He would rarely, if ever, cross the road that led into the compound. With few limitations, he was master of all he surveyed. Up to the road was about as much as he surveyed, and he seemed happy with that.

Snarffle had a plane ticket to the states, obtained much more easily than our respective DEROS orders. Frank Croty, whom Snarffle adopted when we moved to Long Binh, was going to take him back with him, to New York City. He chidingly asked me if I wanted to take Snarffle home with me. I didn't take him very seriously. I already had two dogs at home, and I could never keep up with his liquor tab. Snarffle would have to go on the wagon, and that might have done him in. Judging from every indication, Frank was intent on taking him home and putting him out to stud. I'm reasonably sure that he made it. Spuds Mackenzie seems to have his eyes.

While we were in Xuan Loc, David Niemeyer somehow adopted a cat. How he obtained it, and kept it, in view of the Vietnamese liking, for cats as a delicacy, had to be a major preoccupation and most prolific accomplishment of his time in Vietnam. For the sake of its survival, he always had to keep a watchful eye on it. He would pamper the cat; treating it better than a lot of people that he worked with. He would also feed it much better than most Vietnamese around there ate- and they ate very well. He would feed it shrimp. The Vietnamese didn't mind too much, for they probably looked on it as a potential meal, and that it should have been taken care of, in the meantime. They would wait. Sometimes, just to harass David, we would tease the cat; or the Vietnamese would smack their lips when they looked at him. Obviously, he spent a lot of time being upset. In his irritation, David would counter by reminding us that Vietnamese also ate dogs, too. We weren't too worried, because Snarffle was probably too ugly to be in any danger. He also looked so strange to them, that they must have considered him supernatural, maybe even one of their reincarnated Buddhist ancestors. Snarf was a celebrity. They were too much in awe of him.

The cat staked out its territory in the hootch, and Snarffle quickly learned to keep his distance, maintaining a reasonable margin of safety. They grew to tolerate each other and had very little disagreement.

David's cat had an admirer, a large, orange, male cat from the Vietnamese compound. This cat was probably more on the wild side, and probably had to spend a lot of time living by his wits, which he seemed to do very well. This was probably what attracted her to him, aside from his possibly being the only other male cat in Xuan Loc City. As a result, letting nature take its course, David's cat would disappear from time to time. David, in his nervous housemother manner, would scold her when she returned, for her disheveled appearance, as the result of her night out, or, in some cases, several days (and nights) out on the town. He would get more irritable than usual when this happened. The cat probably served as a vent for his feelings, good and bad. He would probably have been even more impossible to live with, if he didn't have that cat for company.

When we left for Long Binh, the cat disappeared again, this time for good. David never said what happened to the cat. Possibly, it ended up in Ba One's stew pot or it set up housekeeping with the orange cat and lived happily ever after. He missed it, but he would never admit that either.

Soot was a late-comer to the compound. Why we needed another dog on the compound, I don't know. Neither did Snarffle. At first, this puppy was a major irritation, with it tagging along, around him all the time, but they soon got along pretty well, and became a part of the unit.

During the Tet season, around the end of January, we acquired a parrot. It was purchased from a Vietnamese boy, who convinced someone that one of the customs of the Tet celebration was to release a bird, probably to symbolize peace and/or freedom. It turned out that the boy literally gave us the bird, for we found out, on a closer examination, that its wings were clipped. We couldn't let it go; the cat would get it, illustrating another link in the Vietnamese food chain. As a result, he became another addition to our growing zoo. It traveled with us, when we stood down at Long Binh.

We even had a praying mantis for a pet, at least for a little while, in the OB shop. He was named Deacon. He didn't seem very difficult to get along with, and he was pretty quiet. We had sort of an accident, one night, while spraying for mosquitoes. He apparently got in the way and started to change color. I had to get him outside and let him go. While he was with us, he was very good company.

It was quite a move, when we packed up and moved to Long Binh. Our pets, combined with the Frenzel Jones menagerie, seemed to present some preliminary problems, with getting along. Hank, the old 25th MIC mascot, didn't immediately hit it off with Snarffle, but they eventually got around to tolerating each other. The animals kept, were probably, reflections of our collective personalities. I think that we had a good group.

2/25'S LAST XUAN LOC OPERATIONS

In February, probably around St. Valentine's Day, it was announced that Xuan Loc Forward would be winding down operations, in preparation for standing down sometime in March. This confirmed what I had hoped for, all along. It meant, most importantly, that I'd be going home, probably a month early. This was the best news that I could possibly have received. I was anxious to see my family again- especially my new family and enjoy all the things that I had missed when I was over here: Toilets, TV, current newspapers, air conditioning and <u>real</u> milk! The prospect of actually going home was starting to become a reality, and it was just overwhelming to think about. I did have to survive another month, in order to go home the way that I wanted to- alive and in one piece.

 I had to keep in mind that there were still people out there who weren't going home and didn't really care if I was and might even try to inadvertently to stop that. I understood that it was nothing personal, but I had decided a long time before that I was going to have my way in this particular situation. I was going to be as careful as I could in considering the circumstances.

 In the meantime, there were still the everyday operations of the OB shop, and the operations, in general of the 2nd Brigade of the 25th Division. Regular operations were continually carried out. Some of the field units had been brought into Xuan Loc Forward for security, ever since the 18th ARVN had left for Cambodia, leaving our positions, extremely vulnerable to whatever was out there at the time. It was debatable whether The18th ARVN's departure was a curse or a blessing. With them around, they presented a larger and more prominent target for any harassment, which some factions felt that they richly deserved, including the NVA and the VC. On the other hand, with our units providing security, at least we had people around that we could better depend on. This also worked so that the 2/25th units would be winding down their operations in the area, and decreasing our responsibility for operations in the Xuan Loc area.

This was also probably a last opportunity for some of the more career-oriented military personnel to go out on one last operation before they left for home. As far as I was concerned, I'd just do what was necessary to survive and not really go out for any extracurricular stunts that could possibly have curtailed my plans of running up the gangplank and jumping on that plane in less than four weeks. Apparently, that wasn't good enough for some individuals, particularly some senior level NCO's who hadn't yet earned their combat infantryman's badge and would never have earned it in the normal circumstances of riding a desk for their respective tours. As far as I was concerned, the people who really deserved to wear that badge were the people who were out there all the time, risking their lives, and routinely taking the worst of the situation. I personally resented that somebody could slip out from behind their desk, on a one-time basis, shoot up a couple of trees and claim to qualify for that particular commendation.

Information on the rear-service groups, was given to the S2 and the other powers that were, to plan an outing to intercept one of these groups in the re-supply of a certain unit, in a certain area. Obviously, the parts of this information that would have shown such an operation to be ineffective were either left out or ignored: The assumption that the Ho Chi Minh Trail was, all the way, from north to south, a wide super highway paved with bamboo, on which re-supply was executed on a train-like schedule, along one designated route, seemed to be deeply imbedded into their psyche. The supply routes were intricate, but not in the way that they had reasoned. It usually happened that if the rear service personnel had detected something going on along the route that they usually took, they would certainly not have taken the chance of losing people or equipment in a toe-to toe encounter with a superior force lying in wait for them. These were not necessarily combat personnel; their mission was to re-supply, and of late, they really had their problems. There were many instances of VC/NVA prisoners and Hoi Chans who claimed that not only was it hard to get equipment, they, many times couldn't, themselves, get enough to eat. These were desperate people, but certainly not stupid people. My half-joking suggestion was to hang around Trang Bang Market, and they would probably show up there. In retrospect, it might not have been far from the truth.

At first, I was at glad that the information that I had been working on for a long time was finally going to be useful. That feeling didn't last for long, however, when I learned that it wasn't necessarily going to be the case. I was partially vindicated in the respect that Larry had given them this information for whatever reason. I'm not sure that he relayed any reservations, regarding the feasibility of the operation. He acknowledged my reservations and reminded me that they were going to do what they wanted, anyway. I also felt that there was just as much an element of danger for them, too: There may possibly be someone waiting for the people who were waiting for them. After all, it was their jungle, and nobody could know it better than them.

This situation was just another reminder of what this particular job was all about, and where it fit in the scheme of things. OB is attached to S2, which makes the evaluations regarding the enemy situation. The OB section chief only has responsibility for what comes out of his shop, and his enlisted personnel have even less of a say as to what will and won't work, in putting together an operation. It wasn't even in the S2's sphere of influence to rule on it. He could only recommend it. It was technically the Brigade commander's responsibility to order it. It isn't clear just who had organized this little expedition; but at least one person that I knew returned with his CIB, whom I feel to this day didn't deserve it. If I were to receive any awards for that particular episode- which I didn't, I'd have returned them. I felt that it was an unnecessary risk of life and waste of equipment. It was one of the few times that I felt ashamed to be part of that unit. I really took it personally.

What I did get out of this particular episode was the feeling that events were not in my control, and the situation was just as complex and unmanageable as before. The feeling, upon arriving, that I could make some significant difference was quickly dissipating, and I was of the feeling that it would be good to shake the dust of this place from my boots, and hope that negotiations and elections would eventually straighten out the situation. I had a lot of doubts about how well that was going to work. I felt most sorry for the people who had trusted us to help them- they really did exist. My major concern was that, in the long run, their association with us, when it came time to reconcile with the other Vietnamese would be a basis for recriminations. I pray for them, to this day.

One of the greatest paradoxes of this particular situation is that the persons that we supposedly came over to help, all political rhetoric aside, were vulnerable to not only the danger and uncertainty of our prosecuting a war around them, that they may or may not have wanted. They were also the ones who were to suffer various recriminations from others, just for having been associating with us.

In trying to make some sense of this war, instances in which close friends have been lost before someone's eyes, at times have been effectively blocked out, so as not to relive the horror of that particular instance. For me, in order to leave here, I had to believe that I had done all that I could do for them, and that whatever else could be done for them would have to be done from home. I felt that I'd have much more control of the situation at home than I'd ever have here- after all, I was there, and I had seen it...Right? People would be interested to get a first-hand account of what was really going on over there- or would they? It was with all sorts of conflicting thoughts, about the people that we were going to leave behind and the people that I was to be reunited with, back home, that I packed my bags for Long Binh and made my preliminary preparations to go home.

XUAN LOC FAREWELL

In the middle of March, as one of the formal procedures of standing down as a unit involved formally presenting the Xuan Loc compound to the Vietnamese. Knowing what it probably degenerated to over the four weeks, since I left it, I wasn't really that excited about going back. I wasn't really that impressed with it from a safety standpoint; but that was where I was ordered to go. I reasoned, however, because of my knowledge of the compound, my chances of surviving the night in that area were far better than someone who had just come in from the field. This had been home, and once back there I didn't mind it at all. I had somehow managed to get a cold, but otherwise, I was all right. As far as I was concerned this would be my idea of a last operation- something that just a few of us got to do. From what we were told, it was probably one of the first of many instances to demonstrate that the South Vietnamese armed forces were gradually taking over the operations that the American forces had previously assumed. What the reality of it was, I had no real way of knowing, for my sources of information were obviously very limited, and I'd have wanted something more than a current copy of <u>Time</u> to base my opinions on. I liked to think that my closer proximity to the situation would have given me more of an insight. I was winding up my tour in Vietnam, not really sure of what I knew. If I did know something, I probably wasn't anything useful to the overall situation.

I was in on what something should be noteworthy, in terms of the history of the 25th Division. This was comparable to the unit coming home from Japan, after its occupation assignment, and Korea, after the Geneva Accords were agreed upon. This was nothing earth shaking, but it was witnessing a comparable event from the most down-to-earth vantage point.

I was dropped off, around mid-day with enough gear, and assurances that there would be sufficient facilities available to spend the night. The mess hall was intact, but it wouldn't take very much to cease operations and shut it down. Arrangements had been made that I'd sleep in the MPs quarters.

I spent the afternoon looking around the compound- or at least, what was left of it. Its emptiness made it look very strange. It looked like a ghost town. The large tower that was located to the rear of the headquarters company building had been completely disassembled. All that was left of this once-familiar site was a large bare spot. The tower and its supporting wires were gone.

The buildings that were used for the billets and shops were empty. I explored some of these buildings with Frank Canoli, from the Imagery Interpretation section. There was always some activity coming out of these places, and now they were all silent, except for the sound of some of the Vietnamese who were, by now, familiar faces in the area.

The perimeter was quiet, except for the goats that routinely kept the vegetation down, especially on the far side of the compound. It was, up to this time, kept fairly neat, by the efforts of the Vietnamese day workers, who were kept on just for that purpose. Probably the reason that it was so neat was that there weren't that many Americans around making a mess. This would be their last day in our employ. It was unlikely that ARVNs would maintain the same arrangement.

A Contradiction of Terms: A 25th Division Analyst's Tour in Vietnam

I really didn't have anything to give them, but before I left the first time, I did give them some photographs that I had taken of Hue, her cousin, and also of Ba One. I was acutely aware that once we were gone, we couldn't be sure of what was going to happen to them. From time to time, among ourselves, we had talked of this, and had to admit that, at best their future was uncertain. I know that David was enamored with Hue, but he would never admit it in a serious sense. I liked to think that he liked her more than his cat, but he acted more upset about losing the cat. I was never really sure of Hue's real age, but she might have been around sixteen or seventeen. I don't think that he wanted any sort of commitment. He had some ideas about staying with the Army past his original enlistment. He seemed to exhibit all the signs of someone who wasn't about to settle down any time soon.

In giving them the photos, I was making them responsible for them. I didn't want them in the hands of someone who might potentially cause them trouble, because of their association with Americans. Even after that I still wondered if that was the right thing to do, and I wish that I had some better picture of them that I had kept. In retrospect, I feel that my reasoning was rather faulty, and the photos might have caused them less trouble in my possession. After that day, I never saw them or heard about them again.

This is yet another instance of things that to this day remaining undone for me concerning the war. In Xuan Loc along with the men that I worked with and went through the tour with, this Vietnamese family was the closest thing that I had to my family at the time. Even though we weren't physically close we were all emotionally tied to one another. Our good byes weren't really outwardly emotional, but I think that they knew that we all cared about what happened to them and that our hearts were with them.

At this point in time, I've no way of knowing what really did happen to them. I know what happened to Xuan Loc, but not to what happened to any of them, personally. Only the present Vietnamese government may be of assistance. I've hopes, but don't expect a major change in policy, in the near future. The mechanics of undertaking such a project, to address that issue, may very much depend on the disposition of the powers that be, in Vietnam at any given time.

For this particular afternoon, Xuan Loc compound was, at least temporarily, out of the war. The rest of the afternoon was spent looking through the empty buildings in the compound. We had two main objectives. The official reason was to make sure that the place looked good when the transition ceremony took place the following day. The other reason, which was much more important, was to make sure that no weapons and supplies were left behind, that could be used against us. Such materials, if found should be accounted for, and in the possession of our personnel. This included food and anything else that might be construed as not in our best interests to leave behind.

I'd have assumed that the Vietnamese would have done some of the major policing operations on their own, and had already carried off whatever they were allowed to take out through the front gate. They mostly carried out boxes of C Rations. My feelings were rather mixed on seeing these things go. Considering my gastronomic experiences of some of those canned items, I wondered if we were really doing them a favor. I'm sure that none of it was wasted. It would probably be the last handout that they would get for a long time.

The Vietnamese were always very resourceful. When it came to improvising and I had no doubt that they would make that food last as long as possible. The ones that I knew were also very good cooks. One of the best meals that I had in Xuan Loc obviously didn't come from the mess hall. (I was a casualty of the mess hall at one point. It occasioned a visit to the dispensary at Husky compound, for stomach problems.)

Shortly before we left, we gave Ba One some extra money to bring some food in from Xuan Loc market, in order to make a real Vietnamese meal for all of us. What she cooked consisted of a variety of cooked vegetables with a little meat. She even supplied the nuoc mam- a fish sauce that seemed to be put on everything. The smell of the concoction was legendary. It actually tasted a lot better than it smelled. We only got a chance to do this once. I wished that we had found out a little sooner, and we could have done it as a matter of routine.

As the day wound down, we went over to the mess hall for the next to last time. Actually, this was one place that I wasn't going to miss at all. Many people who have been here have bitter memories of combat and destruction. My most bitter memories were of the mess hall in terms of what they did to the food, and how they served it. This was one thing that I don't think I will ever miss. The food that night; however, wasn't too bad at all the prospect of their going out of business probably tempered my usual contempt for them. I believe, as an extra added precaution, I had taken some sort of junk food ration with me, just for survival's sake. I wasn't about to go out starving.

Our dinner guests were the units that had been sent to Xuan Loc to secure the compound, until it was officially turned over to the ARVNs. They seemed much louder and ill-at-ease than any of the regular people that we normally had here. Apparently, to them this was a strange place, and they didn't know what to expect- which was understandable.

On the compound, when this was home, we were familiar with every sound that emanated from the outside. Even if there were sounds that we didn't like, at least we knew about them and took them in stride. All through the night, the units watching the perimeter were busier and more upset than any other bunker guard combination that we ever had here, and that included the night that they mortared Husky compound, or the night that one of the tower bunkers had burned down. I didn't hear anything out of the ordinary going on outside, but these guys in here were yelling and wanted to shoot at everything. It was like they had never seen Vietnamese before. Everything they heard gave them a reason to treat it as an alert. This was rather awkward, especially early in the evening, when there were Vietnamese all over the place, with Xuan Loc City being less than a mile away. As far as I could tell, there was nothing out there that was going to get them. They were spooking themselves. These were presumably men who had come from the field and they must have been out there way too long. They weren't doing too well in here. If there were any VC around, they probably could have been captured quite easily, for they would have been rolling around on the ground, laughing uncontrollably. They wouldn't even have had to come close to cause any confusion; these guys brought it with them. Probably the safest place they could have been was in front of one of our bunkers. This group didn't seem to have it together. I really couldn't figure out what their problem was.

I found a bunk in the MP headquarters, and went to bed probably around eleven or twelve, listening to the radio and any music that was playing. When I did fall asleep, I slept pretty well. I must have woken up about once or twice, because of all the commotion, on the perimeter. It didn't bother me too much. I felt that this was the safer place to be. Those guys out there seemed to be set on shooting themselves, and I thought it best to stay out of the way. This must have been how they survived in the environment they were used to- I don't know how they survived, but in some bizarre manner, it apparently worked for them. When I left Long Binh, I thought that I'd be the one that was going to be scared, but it was quite the reverse.

When morning came, I went to shower and got something to eat at the mess hall, one last time. After this meal, the rest of the gear in the mess hall was probably cleaned (for the first time in a long time) and packed away. The Vietnamese help was sent off with the last of the food that could be carried off, and the compound was ready for one last going over. This was the most important one, because it was going to be the last.

The afternoon before, the place looked in decent shape, but after what I had heard the night before, I wasn't so sure. I didn't really feel as close to these guys and I did with other groups, and I sensed that the feeling was mutual. As a part of the intelligence contingent, I didn't wear rank insignia. In this case, I was advised not to. In this subculture, they probably had contempt for both officers and CID, of which I was neither, but perceived as one, the other, or both. I was advised to keep them guessing, for my own safety. Lieutenants Mitchum and O'Neil arrived a little later in the morning, in preparation for the ceremony, and Frank and I were getting ready for one last look at the area. We picked up some trash, here and there; it didn't make any sense to get into a fight over that. What couldn't be ignored, in the sector that I was responsible for, was a grenade that was left in a bunker. I was advised to keep it for obvious reasons. I really would have liked to have held on to it for a while, because, in that way, I knew where it was. Under the circumstances, there might have been rather a curious photograph taken of a soldier standing at parade rest, in the formation, with a live grenade in his hand. The suggestion that it be taken home as a souvenir, really didn't appeal to me either. It wasn't one of the items that I wanted to collect, and I also had this thing about not keeping any government property. The only thing that I really wanted to collect was my body, which I wanted to run up that plane's gangway, in less than a week. I didn't want anything to interfere with that.

I found a sergeant in charge of the platoon in the area and confronted him about the grenade. He had someone to take it and put it away. I heard some back talk about it, and I mentioned that I'd rather be handing it to him, than to be playing catch with a VC. He mentioned to me behind my back of course, how he would have liked to give it back, but I tactfully ignored him and got out of the vicinity. I mentioned the incident to Lt. Mitchum, and he also talked to the sergeant. There was nothing more heard from them after that and the area was ready for the formal ceremony, which was to be held around noontime. This was the last official ceremony to be held at Xuan Loc Forward.

One of the historic events that I use to mark this date in history is the first heavyweight championship fight between Muhammad Ali and Joe Frazier. That was another main reason that I wanted to stay in Long Binh, at this particular time. We had agonized through several of Ali's fights, in his comeback for the championship. He had beaten Oscar Bonavena, and he felt that he was ready for Joe Frazier. After all the anticipation, everyone wanted to be somewhere, to keep track of this fight. I couldn't wait to get back to Long Binh, again. The fight was going to start about twelve or twelve-thirty and was going to be broadcast over AFVN. Fortunately, someone did bring a radio, so we could listen to it as soon as we were on our way back to Xuan Loc Forward.

Although I may not have completely appreciated the significance of our turning over the Xuan Loc compound to the South Vietnamese, I was aware, in any case, that this was a prime example of what had been promised to facilitate Vietnamization. At least in a small way scaling down American operations was becoming a reality. How the rest of South Vietnam was doing, I had no real way of knowing, from here. At around this time, talks about elections were making the rounds. I held that out as a good sign, or at least one of the indicators that the Vietnamese was really going to be on their own. How long they were going to last, on their own was still a matter of conjecture. I personally hailed these moves as steps in the right direction. These conditions had apparently eased my conscience enough to not worry about several years down the line, and to just be satisfied with what was happening now.

At noontime, we assembled in the road, in front of the headquarters building, and waited for the South Vietnamese Army contingent to arrive. It was a bright, sunny day, and the compound never looked better. It was quiet, and peaceful. The wind could actually be heard, in the trees, and even birds could be heard. Conditions of this sort, when we were operating here were non-existent. With our own jobs, the artillery, choppers and assorted vehicles, combined with whatever the other side was doing at the time, things like this weren't part of our real world, and hence forgotten about. It seemed to be a sign that the war was really winding down for us. Looking around at the trees and the beautiful blue sky, I got the feeling that we got them back again, after so many colorless days, which we plodded through, one at a time. This was my own personal celebration of life, and I reveled in it for the rest of the time that I was there. The conversation was easy, and the anticipation of handing this place over intact, made me glad that I could be a part of it. I didn't feel that way the day before, or even the night before, but for now, I could now put all that aside.

We talked about the technical/administrative vulnerability of the compound at that particular time. I joked that within a few minutes, it would be out of our hands, one way or another!

The Vietnamese arrived shortly after noon, and we got into a quiet formation in front of the company area. Actually, it wasn't even a matter of being called to attention, and we casually stood by, and watched what turned out to be a very informal proceeding. It was a very short, quiet ceremony, there were no bands, speeches or military drills. The officers in charge of the respective American and Vietnamese units saluted each other, there was a little small talk, some smiles and then it was over. Military tradition on this occasion was only apparent in the official passing of the installation to The ARVNs and was in following what was probably, in simple military protocol.

The symbolism of the occasion was less apparent in that as part of an American unit operating in South Vietnam, we had in at least this small part of Vietnam, fulfilled what we had been sent there to do. It was great to be part of that. What history would interpret, in a grander scheme, in years to come, wasn't really important then. From everything that I could see, from here, we had won and we were going home.

This was the closest that most of us who were involved in this war came to see it brought to a successful conclusion and had any reason to feel that we prevailed. My concern for the Vietnamese, who would take responsibility again, never really lessened. I obviously was unsuccessful in my resolve to not get involved any more than was necessary. My curiosity and concern for what ultimately happened to them, and especially my friends, continues to this day.

PART IV- LONG BINH AND HOME

Camp Frenzel-Jones

The move was made from Xuan Loc to Long Binh, around the beginning of March. The 25th MID would still be in operation until the official stand down of the Second Brigade, which was to take place in about two weeks. With the impending stand down, the pace of activities was considerably slower, giving us more time to get to know our counterparts who comprised Xuan Loc Rear. Time could also be taken to explore the massive Long Binh complex; which, beforehand, I had seen very little of. I still don't think that I saw much more of it, in the three weeks that I was there.

The routine at CFJ was similar to the ones in the other places that I had been. The only difference here was that forward progress was measured here, in how well the operations could be scaled down- ideally to nothing- by the given amount of time that we had left here as a unit. Details still had to be done, but they were really nothing major, and nothing to fret about. Actually, I had about as much leisure time as I could stand. With my departure drawing near, time seemed to drag. I was used to keeping occupied with one thing or another. I'd use that free time to write, wander around to see what everyone else was doing, and get ready to finally go home. Once the morning details were out of the way, and any special assignments were taken care of, the rest of the day was free.

The personnel in Xuan Loc had made a world of their own. They obviously had their own routines, which included DEROS tans, side-trips inside and outside of Long Binh, and their own style of partying.

The Frenzel-Jones Compound had two adjacent features: an old Vietnamese cemetery, and a small movie house. The compound, itself, was very compact, and probably took up a miniscule part of the huge base camp. Being unfamiliar with the area, I usually stayed close to the compound, except for minor probing of nearby adjacent areas. If someone were going out on an errand it wasn't improper to tag along, just to keep from going stir-crazy. As a result, most of what I saw was from going out on some of the errands that required a jeep. Because of the size of the complex, this was done out of necessity, rather than convenience. I wasn't really used to this way of life because of the compactness of the Xuan Loc compound. This size difference, between the Xuan Loc compound and the Long Binh complex, took a lot of getting used to.

The mess hall attached to Headquarters Company was located across a large open area, which, at first glance, looked rather overwhelming. It was worth the walk, because the food was every bit as the food at the 25th MP mess, back at Chu Chi. It was, as far as I was concerned, the best thing next to being home.

Where this compound was located, in relation to everything else in Long Binh, I had next to no idea, and I hoped that I really wouldn't have the time left in country to figure it out, being two weeks short. I was content to be able to find my way between the mess hall, the MID building and the movie house. I couldn't wander out of the base camp if I tried; I didn't even know where the gate was. The change was, at first, very disorienting.

The CFJ compound itself was fairly compact. Like other areas, except for the mess hall it was essentially self-contained. Because of the vast expanse of the Long Binh complex, going to a restaurant or a PX, we usually had to get a ride on whatever was going that way. Considering the scaled-down expectations of what was considered to be normal living with the basic necessities, everything that was needed was contained within the limits of the Long Binh Complex.

In augmenting t cursory description, from my first visit, the main building was the icehouse-type structure, and was the central area of activity of the 2/25th MIC. It didn't have any windows, and it had a large loading dock door. In this building, were some the billets, the map room and some of the section offices the changing conditions of the stand down routinely altered the accommodations. At one point, the interrogation section commandeered the room that I was in for one of their sessions. Over my protests they maintained that they had a right to the rooms for the time that they needed them. The room assignments changed so rapidly, that the interrogation section took for granted that they could take advantage of the chaos and use anyplace they wanted to operate from. I didn't much care where I was assigned, just as long as I didn't have to move my furniture every few days. It was bad enough having to do it on the major moves.

Operations of the 585th MID, in this configuration were very scaled down, in comparison to our operations at Xuan Loc. While an OB shop, of sorts, was maintained- compressed into the same general area as the other sections. Daily briefings or even informal briefings were not part of the normal routine. Assignments in the shop were given as needed, and unit assignments were more likely to be given than the actual shop assignments.

The possible reason for not giving a formal shop briefing was because of the possible inconvenience it might cause in the same general area. The most probable reason was that there may not been a lot of enemy activity to report. With the tactical units standing down and other support units that were no longer needed packing up, not a lot was happening.

A Contradiction of Terms: A 25th Division Analyst's Tour in Vietnam

The shear anticipation of going home was the main order of business, and little else was important. The concept of going home was rather mind-boggling and took a little getting used to. After talking about it for almost the whole time, the reality of it was just starting to be manifested. My thoughts on it, other than general goals of getting on with my life, of family and school, were not really mapped out. I felt that I should at least be allowed to savor my primary accomplishment of surviving this place and take time to appreciate a lot of the things that I had missed along the way. Being back with Betty was what I was most looking forward to. In being married, I had been away from her longer than I had been with her. The situation was changed now, because of our daughter. I was a father now, and we were a family. What it would really be like, I could only guess. I looked forward to the time that I'd see her for the first time. I wasn't sure what to expect. I felt that I'd be stepping into someone else's life. At any rate, I knew that life would never be the same.

I was also told, that in that year, I may have changed, and to be patient with the people that I was to come back to. I wasn't sure of why this was said; but it did make me wonder to what extent that would be true. I wondered if the changes were in me or the world to which I was returning. I was anxious to find out. My anticipation of returning home far outweighed any worries about what it would be like. I was ready.

Frenzel-Jones Personalities

Most of the others were not all that noteworthy, probably because of the short amount of time that we actually spent with them. Most were friendly, and tolerated us, but others remained in their own group. Others had their own reasons for maintaining this type of social interaction.

There was a diverse mix of personalities encountered on The FJC compound. The people who were members of Xuan Loc Forward were obviously the ones that I knew best. Larry Moog, David Niemeyer, Will Guhman, and the Lt's Mitchum and O'Neil came over with me from Xuan Loc. Assorted members of counterintelligence, imagery interpretation and the interrogation sections also contained members who had been in Xuan Loc Forward. Most of us were associated with 25th MIC, in Cu Chi. That was, in relative terms, a long association. Mr. Brown, and Neil Hill, whom I had known from the beginning of assignment in Cu Chi. Many of the others, I didn't really have a lot of contact with, until now. These others may have come from far-flung parts of our former area of operations. Personnel rotations, because of the twelve and eighteen-month duty tours, also brought other members into the unit. We didn't really meet until now. It was one of those cases in which chance, rather than any grand design brought us together, for better or for worse.

The scenery, and the situation outside of the compound was, many times of secondary importance to what was going on within our own perimeter. The social interaction, between these factions, at times left a lot to be desired. A lot of time was spent feeling each other out. Our worlds, more often than not, clashed. Some friendships did result from this unit combination, but it wasn't always the case.

The only people that I really knew here were the ones that had been with me at Xuan Loc Forward, and the frequent visitors from Xuan Loc rear, like Terry Eways and Larry de Montebello. The others were not all that visible and were relatively unknown.

Terry, in the real world, sold rugs, by trade, with a specialty in Persian rugs. He would always be ready to discuss what and what not to buy in the rug market. His future seemed geared to taking up this rug-dealing business, as soon as he got back. I have every confidence that he did. He seemed to have a good mind for business, and he was very knowledgeable in his field. He was very easy-going and was a frequent visitor to Xuan Loc Forward. Although he was from Philadelphia, He had a western drawl, like the Monkee's Mike Nesmith. He was always very comical. He was another one who liked to do impressions in various dialects and was always one of the stars of the compound. He took great pains to educate us on the street mannerisms of the South Philadelphians, and survival in the big city- should we ever find ourselves in such a circumstance.

Although Terry could hold his own as a stand-up comedian, it was Larry De Montebello who was the clown of Xuan Loc Rear. Larry would do skits on his experiences in basic training. His favorite was a drill sergeant who fractured his name into "Dee-mot-tab'-a-low." He routinely referred to himself as "Fop 2", in deference the Frenchman from 25th MIC.

Xuan Loc Forward had a company clerk, who was with us at forward for a short time. He was a shady character who always looked like he was up to something, all the time- and he usually was. He was one of the few people that Larry Moog advised all of us to avoid. He seemed very street-wise, in a sense that he was adept in associating himself with the darker sides of our involvement, here, such as drugs, prostitution and procuring contraband. He was known to use people, and I became very conscious of it in my own experience with him.

My feeling about the influence of this person was a fairly simplistic one. I wanted nothing to delay my leaving here. If it did, I was going to be more than upset. I perceived him as my last barrier to getting on that plane. I was going to watch him very carefully.

Diversions

Because of the scaling-down of operations in 25th MID, there wasn't a lot to do except to move furniture, and quarters and to maintain a charge-of-quarters schedule that we all were to take a turn. I had it on one occasion and maintained it in a somewhat party-atmosphere of the main headquarters building. Although, it was all very relaxed and there was almost no supervision by officers and senior NCOs, it was almost ideal for some of the individuals who looked forward to such things. On my watch, however, my position was respected- partly out of their knowing my sense of duty about these things, and partly because the Xuan Loc Forward personnel weren't quite sure of what to expect. I meant to keep them guessing, if necessary, until the plane door had closed behind me, and I was safely out over the South China Sea. That's how much I really trusted them. Their behavior toward me, from the start, had helped me to foster this attitude. I wasn't invited to some of their trips to Saigon, or to any of the market places- probably because they had been where they shouldn't have been and brought back things that they didn't really want me to know about. I didn't really feel left out. I felt that as long as I could do what I wanted to do-, which was to pack for home, I didn't much care what they did or where they went. As a unit, and with few exceptions, the personnel of the forward and rear were never really together long enough, to form any lasting bonds of friendship and probably just didn't seem so inclined. Neither side was inclined to change that. If peer pressure was a motivation for this, it didn't really affect me that much. I was, by this time, used to being on the outside, and free to do one of the few things that I enjoyed in this situation, which was to write, hope and plan for how I was going to live my life back in the world. Little else mattered. I devoted all my attention to getting out of there.

I did make one last attempt to get some of those large crabs from one of the outside markets. Routine trips were made to Cholon, Tan San Nut and Saigon. I'd ask, routinely to bring back some of them so that we could see how they tasted with the Old Bay Seasoning that was sent to me- too late to do any good at Cu Chi. My idea was to make a crab feast part of the send-off ceremonies. This never materialized. In the life that these guys were attuned to, "crabs" registered as buzzword for venereal diseases. A lot of kidding was associated with this, and my idea was never taken seriously. There was a barrier of ignorance that couldn't be penetrated. I tried unsuccessfully to describe how good this was at Cu Chi.

As far as they were concerned, if it couldn't be smoked drank or humped, it served no useful function. This incident only served to worsen my attitude toward them. It was one of my biggest disappointments of my mercifully short experience in Long Binh. My feelings were buoyed by the knowledge that I wasn't going to be there for too much longer. On the balance, there was really no love lost between us. One of my resolutions, on any return to Vietnam, was to pack the Old Bay seasoning and show the Vietnamese what they have been missing all these years! I Think Phillips Sea Food, later effectively took a lucrative variation of my idea, in later years- so much for my million-dollar idea!

Some nights were spent in the movie house, which was adjacent to the compound. It wasn't a very large structure, and it didn't really have the atmosphere of the open-air theaters in other places, but it served the purpose of getting out of the company area for a while, and relief from the stuffiness of our headquarters building. Being in such close quarters, I soon realized that we were getting each other's way. There was little quiet when I wanted to sleep. Bull sessions were carried on into early morning. It wouldn't have mattered, except that, in being so close together, it was a major annoyance.

On one occasion, coming back from the movie house, I walked into one of their parties. This wasn't a normal party. In this instance, there were drugs involved. I was surprised that this was being done in such a blatant manner, by people that I thought that I knew. Being in what seemed like a very small minority, I got out of there and went back to the movie house and watched the next feature.

When I returned, everything seemed back to normal. The people that knew me knew that I wasn't pleased with their lack of discretion. They must have known that there would be no one in authority there that night- so that they would be free to act on their own. I had long-since resolved that if anyone were to do something like that, I didn't want it to involve me. I was well aware that they were going to do what they wanted, anyway, so I stopped getting upset about it. With none of us being responsible for security in this stand down situation, this was apparently taken as their chance to do something like this. The guys that I went through the tour with knew this about me, and we usually let each other go our own ways. They also had to know I was upset about it and would show it in my own ways.

Individuals of the Xuan Loc Rear contingent didn't really know me, however. One individual approached me about it, at a time when I was still pretty much upset by it. I never intended to carry the matter any further. The people who knew me already knew how I felt, and what I'd or wouldn't do about it. I admonished this person by saying that if he knew me at all; he wouldn't even really have to bring it up. As much as I disliked him, I felt that no useful purpose could be served by making an accusation that probably wouldn't stick, and also spoil any chances of getting out of here on time.

My words seemed to make him even more ill at ease. He <u>didn't</u> know me, and now it really bugged him. For the first time that I had ever seen him, he was speechless. I knew when I left him; he had become even more dangerous than ever. He wanted to insure my silence. For my part, I didn't hide my feelings very well. I had this sinking feeling that he was desperate enough to create circumstances that would be a means to that end. Since he was probably one of the controllers of the paperwork that would get me out of here, he was potentially my biggest obstacle. He tested me, but he really had no advantage to press. He could only work on my mind; and my mind wasn't set on any sort of one-ups-man-ship or revenge; I just wanted to go home. He had to know, however, that if I found out that my departure from Vietnam was delayed by an hour, I'd be all over him, and I'd use that delay to make his life miserable. This wasn't really the standoff that he implied. I'd make sure that he would lose. It was bad enough to have to put up with something that I didn't agree with, let alone try to coerce me into condoning it. The circumstance of being involved in a war was bad enough, but no one, until then, seriously suggested that I should regress to adolescence, where peer pressure was a dominating force. He did guess wrong about me and he knew how faulty his reasoning sounded as soon as the words left his mouth.

In the time remaining there, I maintained a healthy distrust for him, and had a tendency to blame any minor snag in my out-processing on him. In several instances, he tried to make a pest of himself, but I faced him down, and after that, he troubled me no more.

Last Operations

By the third week of March, I was more ready than ever to get out of here. The time was so close; it was really getting to me. The time just dragged. There was nothing going on, except sporadic assignments and a little miscellaneous paperwork.

I felt that I was so close to leaving that I wrote my last letter from here on the 17th of March. [I was too excited to write a long letter.] I felt that I'd beat some of these letters home. I wouldn't have minded that at all.

On several occasions, I was offered a helicopter ride, on a mail run. This was also at a time when the NVA and the VC were having an open season of Hueys and light observation helicopters. I declined, but said I'd go if ordered. With that, the matter was carried no further. I was bored, but not *that* bored. I felt that it would be prudent to keep my feet on the ground for the few days that I had left here. I wasn't really inclined to take unnecessary risks.

    I did, however, get out, one more time. On one of these final evenings with 25th MIC, Frank Croty stopped by and asked me if I wanted to go with him to the Hospital at Long Binh, to talk to a wounded NVA prisoner. Going stir-crazy around here, with the minutes seeming like hours, I jumped at the chance to do something that would take the edge off of the waiting to head for home.

Taking a jeep to the Hospital, we arrived in time to find out that the NVA soldier was in surgery, and would probably be better able to talk, in the morning. While we were in Long Binh proper, we stopped over to 585th MID, at II Field Force. On the way, we passed the replacement depot that I'd be leaving from very shortly. Not far from there, we spotted a group of Vietnamese, near the gate. When they saw us, coming out of the dark, they scattered. It was one of those situations in which you just want to say: "Nawww!" but, there was a report to that effect, indicating a small group, in that area, at that time, and that the replacement depot had taken several rounds of mortar fire.

When we arrived at II Field Force, we went over to the EM club. This club was the largest that I had ever seen. They seemed to have all the comforts of home. Aware that my concept of comfortable living had eroded, in the past year, that was the impression that I had. Music, TV and food seemed to be everywhere, and that was my measure of comfortable living at that time. It looked like a lot of fun. While I was there, I tried to look up Jim Maddox, a classmate from the 70-RA-2 class, at Fort Holabird.

When Admiral McCain visited our S2 shop in December, Terry Herweh, another classmate from my RA class, accompanied them. We got to talk for a while and got some information of who went where. Jim Maddox was assigned with him at II Field Force, and I thought that I'd take the opportunity to find him. From what I knew about him, he would most be here. My hunches were correct. I did find Terry; but on this night, Jim wasn't there. I did feel good that I made the attempt. We stayed around for a little while, and then headed back to the Frenzel-Jones compound, arriving about 11:30. I was grateful for the time out; it also gave me the chance to round out my experiences, and a chance to touch bases with some former associates. I don't think that I appreciated them enough, when I was going to school with them at Holabird, but they were links to the world that I was about to return to.

I ended up doing one of the things that I said that I wouldn't do, in taking any unnecessary risks; being out after dark in a non-secure area; but something inside told me that I had to be there, and felt secure out there with someone that I trusted. This was the last time out during my tour. The only thing left to do was to get ready and head for home.

...On My Way Back Home...

You and I have memories
Longer than the road
That stretches out ahead

Two of Us

The Beatles

On the 21st of March, I got the news that I had waited for: orders for home. I got the assignment at Fort Holabird that I requested. Before this, I was informally out-processing, as much as could be done, up to that time. Now, this was for real. With actual out-processing, there were several things that had to be taken care of. Once these were accomplished, I was free to leave Frenzel Jones, and head for the replacement depot. It was really difficult to comprehend that once I completed this administrative scavenger hunt, I'd be on my way back to the states. The catch was in completing the list.

On the list of things to do would be to have my shot record up to date, to clear the medical area, the personnel office, the bank and get a security debriefing from the OB chief, Lt. Mitchum. In addition, I also had to figure out what to send home and what to give away. My furniture, books and everything accumulated over the past year had to either be packed up or given away.

A Contradiction of Terms: A 25th Division Analyst's Tour in Vietnam

Getting packed and getting rid of the things that I wasn't taking home was probably the job that took the most energy. Avoiding the accumulated clutter of furniture, papers, souvenirs, and various odds and ends, seemed to be a never-ending battle. I had to seriously think of what I was going to use, when I got home. Souvenirs were really not on my priority list. My sense of things historical wasn't very well developed. Some of the things, therefore, that I did leave behind, I wish, now, that I hadn't. One item, that none of my associates would have wanted me to leave behind, I did. The guitar that I bought from Joe Fishman, at Cu Chi. I gave away. It was too large and fragile to ship by surface mail. I could have carried it on the plane, but I had, by then, resolved that I was going to travel as light as possible. I also felt that I didn't play it well enough to be carrying it around, and neither did most of my associates. I gave it to someone who I felt would make the best use of it. I felt that if I should get the urge to play the guitar again, I'd use my brother's.

I had accumulated a fair number of books and papers, like the <u>Stars and Stripes.</u> Only one issue of the paper survives in my collection, preserved only because it had photos of the Ali-Frazier fight. I had no idea, at the time that I'd be using them for any serious research. The story of that guitar is significant. I knew Joe Fishman, mainly from the OB hootch at Cu Chi. I associated him not so much with the job as the musical accompaniment of our billet. He was pretty much fond of <u>Creedence Clearwater Revival</u> and had his own parodies of "Bad moon rising" and assorted folk and country pieces like "Stewball", popularized by <u>Peter, Paul and Mary</u>. He mentioned that he was associated with Country Joe and the Fish, although he was obviously not Country Joe nor one of the Fish! I had no idea at the time Country Joe's import and notoriety in anti-war circles and operated out of naivety when Joe would go into his act, but it was fun! He tried to teach me some chords on the guitar, which probably caused much suffering within earshot, but we (at least me and Joe) had a good time with it. Try as I could,

I got next to no encouragement and my compatriots preferred that I stick to writing and chess! He sold me his guitar before he left, and I kept it with me till the standdown at Long Binh.

In these circumstances, a lot of us had the same problem, in that we were trying to get rid of a lot of excess baggage, all at the same time. As a remedy to this, a central place was designated to put such items, and whoever wanted anything from this pile was welcome to it. For the things that I didn't want to take home, I wanted to give first preference to people that I knew. This idea got to be a little too much for them and for me; therefore, a lot of the things that I had went into that pile.

Somehow, just before I left, everything that I didn't need immediately was either packed for delivery by surface mail or given away. I only had what was necessary to carry. I still don't know how this was done in time to leave, but it was. I guess that these things have a way of taking care of themselves.

With what I perceived to be the worst of the out-processing over, I went over to the administrative section to gather up my paperwork. I was surprised that it didn't take as long or was as much trouble as when I arrived in April. Everything seemed to check out, and I cleared that area in what I perceived was record time.

On the morning of the day that I cleared FJC, I went to the bank to close out my account. I was probably all smiles, while doing this. I started to feel that I was really leaving here. I chatted with the teller, a pretty Vietnamese girl, telling her all about my going home, and that this was one of the last things that I had to do here. We wished each other well and I was soon on my way back to the compound.

The security debriefing was to be with Lt. Mitchum. I thought that it was going to be a big deal. This turned out to be just an administrative formality. It was just an admonition to not discuss anything classified. With that he just signed the checklist and wished me good luck. This left one place to clear.

The medical clearing was supposed to involve picking up records and making sure that my shot record was up to date. I was given a supply of white a tablets, and big orange pills, for protection against malaria I was given enough to take for the next six weeks,

I had to get an x-ray as part of the medical clearing. I could live a long life- if I could avoid becoming a war casualty. It seemed to take forever clearing this place. They didn't seem to want to let me go. In the meantime, while I was waiting, I gave them a urine specimen. I was told later, that this was to test for any drugs in my system. I could have told them that there wasn't anything that the Army didn't put there in the first place, but they, probably had to find out for themselves. I really had no worry about that. My only concern was the time that all this was taking.

It seemed to take forever for someone to read the x-ray. The cause for the delay turned out to be the result of a typical Army foul-up. The NCO who took the x-ray probably wanted to give me a rough time. It had been a rough year, and I had weathered many things, and if it was just him that stood between that plane, and me he didn't have a prayer. I wasn't going to sit quietly. He felt he had to be sure that I hadn't contracted anything in Vietnam. If I did, I'd have to stay. Up to this time, I was just taking things as they came, just going along with the program. It was getting really late in the afternoon, and I started to get really concerned that I wasn't going to clear the post in time to go the replacement depot that night.

The only thing that I had contracted was a bad attitude, fully realized when I tried to clear the medical facility. I finally did get to see a doctor, a very pleasant and attractive lady, who saw no problem at all with my records. She apologized that the NCO had made a mistake. [Hey! I was willing to forgive and forget! Just let me out of here!]

At around 4:30, I arrived back at the compound. I was assured that if I could get my gear, I could get to the replacement depot in time for supper. This was the moment in which I had a momentous choice to make. I really wouldn't be on the plane any sooner; but, for me, I had to know that I was on my way.

I reserved very little time for goodbyes. I had arrived back on the compound around suppertime, and there were relatively few people on the compound to say goodbye to. The few people that were left to wish me well weren't all that good at goodbyes, anyway. Neither was I.

I remembered that, in Cu Chi, when we would give MIC members a big send-off. The Chinese restaurant would be rented, and a party would be conducted like the Friar's Roast. It was always a lot of fun. I always wonder what it would be like when I left Vietnam. Now that the time had arrived, I wasn't sure of how I felt. My send-off was a quiet one. Some of the people here, I'd probably never see again- and in some cases, that was ok with me. Others, who had really made a difference, I'd miss them very much, and I will carry their spirit with me always. Most of them, however, had gone home before me, and there were very few from the old unit; that still were here to carry on.

Will Guhman, David and Lt. Mitchum were present, but; I'm not sure who else was there from the old group. I knew that I'd see David, again. He got an assignment at Holabird.

I was in a fog, trying to believe that this was happening. I wanted to get out, just in case that I was dreaming, before I found out that this wasn't happening. It was rather a subdued celebration, of sorts. There was no fanfare, but I had a feeling of great accomplishment. I had survived, and I was really on the way home.

In my own excitement, I detected fairly little enthusiasm on the part of the almost unknown members of the compound. Most of the people that I had spent my tour with were gone. The people that were left probably had next to no idea of what I had gone through. I did understand that there was little to be excited about unless you were the one going home. Rubbing it in, however, wasn't my style.

It wasn't as if I was leaving a unit that I could write back to or see again. The 2/25 was packing its bags for the long-awaited trip back to Hawaii, and some of these units wouldn't even have a need to exist. There was little semblance of unity and military tradition evident, and my state of mind was such that, I didn't much care. What I did notice, as a last gesture, was very moving, although I tried to play it down.

Our first sergeant had been with us at Xuan Loc from the beginning. He was the last person on the compound that I talked to, as I headed for the door. He wished me well. He told me that he was glad I was there. I had always been on good terms with him, and he was always fair in his dealings with us. He was always there whenever we had any administrative problems, and he would stick up for us, always. I even got a couple of driving lessons from him. He physically resembled one of the Oriole greats, Boog Powell. I never told him that- I always assumed that he was an Atlanta Braves fan.

As I shook hands with him and headed for the Jeep, I felt that he was still standing there, which seemed out of character, but then I realized what that was about. I didn't really look back. I let him have his moment. He was one who I truly respected and would miss.

REPLACEMENT DEPOT

I arrived at the replacement depot around suppertime. I checked in and got something to eat. The pace here, was much more relaxed. I had, in my journey back, figuratively, cleared the tower. There was really nothing to do that night, except to try on a new feeling of freedom. There was good food, music via AFVN and other miscellaneous sources. There was a little club with a musical trivia contest in progress, and minor personal celebration of the journey home. It was a very special night, one to be savored quietly.

The stay in the replacement depot was like a vacation in itself. Although all of us in one way or another had come to establish our own routine, this was preferred; this was what we aspired to- going home. It was like a whole new world- and we hadn't even gone anywhere yet. Right here was the R & R, and farewell part, all rolled into one. It was most appropriate that I'd be celebrating it with strangers- and yet they weren't really strangers. We had all gone through a powerful life-changing experience. We were tired, but it was a good tired.
Even though we were still here, it was a time to start putting this tour behind us- if we could.

    In a music trivia contest, I won a food prize- a big can of caramel corn or something like that, which I shared all around when I returned to my barracks. I'll always be grateful to John Lennon for <u>Old Brown Shoe</u>. I couldn't recall winning anything before this- (Except this trip to Vietnam!)

A Contradiction of Terms: A 25th Division Analyst's Tour in Vietnam

Larry Moog had transferred to the replacement depot, shortly after I did. We would out-process together, and he would be on the plane with me back to California. He seemed very subdued; I was never really sure of why. It couldn't have been that he would miss being here- or could it? Somehow, I couldn't see him at home anywhere else but here. Perhaps, he was starting to realize, for himself, the impact that he was leaving here, too. Here, he had established, for himself such a leisurely routine, that I really couldn't see him doing anywhere else. Before this, I always felt thought that he could make himself at home anywhere, now I wasn't so sure. I hoped, for his sake, that he could make the adjustment. None of us were really sure of what was in store for us, when we actually did get home.

The next day, processing involved getting scheduled on the actual flight out of here and finding the board that would show when our designated flight would be ready. We also had to make sure that our records were in order. We were also instructed as to what we could and couldn't take with us.

War trophies such as weapons were stringently regulated. Any automatic weapons were contraband, other captured weapons had to be registered, and disabled before they were allowed to be transported at all. The only things that I brought back were not weapons of war, but medical instruments. I brought back, for my father, a hemostat with Russian markings. Another hemostat had Chinese characters, and a pair of scissors was marked as coming from East Germany. In my own quiet way, even if I were never to speak or write a word of what happened in Vietnam, I at least wanted to make the statement, in a subtle way, that we were not just fighting Viet Cong and North Vietnamese. They had a lot of help from the Communist-Block countries. In spite of the rift between Russia and China, they received massive aid from both of them, as well as the other Communist countries.

The North Vietnamese were very shrewd and it was to their credit that they could solicit aid from both Communist factions, and not really be beholding to either one of them. They depicted their cause as a noble and worthwhile one, and something that would be beneficial to Communism, regardless of the form in which it was perceived. They did it quite effectively. They even used the actions of American demonstrators to depict that their cause as a just one. It made me wonder from time to time, what kind of a world I was returning to. It was evident that we were actively disengaging ourselves from this war; how long that was going to take, and what was ultimately going to happen, one could only guess. My guesses, were, unfortunately correct.

We were required to have our urine tested for drugs, which seemed to be part of the accepted routine by this time. They had, in the course of the year, asked for almost everything else- so, why not? This was a precursor of the attitude that prevailed, about returning servicemen from Vietnam.

One of the most uplifting things that happened to me on the last day in the replacement depot was the issuing of a class "A" uniform. The situation was far different now than when we had left the United States. The jungle fatigues that I had grown so used to over the past eleven months were not to be the thing that the well-dressed American soldier would be sporting back to Oakland. That was a major boost for the morale.

We were invited, just before we left, to donate our uniforms to the South Vietnamese who would have need of them. I readily took them up on the offer, and even threw in my hat, which I later wished that I hadn't. At the time I was anxious to get rid of everything that held me to this country, right down to my clothes. It seemed like a good idea at the time. I found out later, that it wasn't really as simple as that.

A Contradiction of Terms: A 25th Division Analyst's Tour in Vietnam

By the middle of the morning, we were all set to go. The flight that I was scheduled for was bound for Travis A.F.B., with one stop in Okada, Japan. I saw, on the board that there was another flight that was for McGuire A.F.B., in New Jersey, which was adjacent to Fort Dix. This flight had one stop, in Alaska. This flight would have ended up much closer to home, but I already was scheduled for the flight to Travis. Knowing the military, like I did, I elected not to complicate matters, by causing problems, especially since everything was going so right. I didn't know about this other flight until it was too late to change it. I didn't mind, because I felt that my return through California would be symbolic. I thought, many times throughout the year, about going back over the San Francisco-Oakland Bay Bridge. It was the way that I had envisioned my return. This would be one of the ways that I'd know that I was home. I wasn't all that concerned about the extra time that it was going to take. I was going home, and that was all that mattered to me.

As for the stop in Japan, I wasn't quite sure of, where, Okada was. It was probably on one of the northernmost of the Japanese Islands. Where it was located, relative to Tokyo or Yokohama, or any of the other major Japanese cities, I wasn't sure. I saw it as another extra-added benefit. Although it was to be one of the shortest of stays, I'll at least have made it to Japan, and any gift shop that happened to be in the vicinity- and I was sure that there would be many.

We finally boarded the buses for the trip to Ben Hoa. It was a beautiful day. The weather, as always, was hot, but not humid, and it was really comfortable. Just outside the gate, at the replacement Depot, some wooden stands were being set up. It turned out that President Thieu was scheduled to speak there around noontime. Although I was, even then, interested in things historical, I wasn't all that disappointed that I was going to miss this. One reason was that I already knew what he was going to say- which wouldn't have been anything new. The other and most obvious reason was that my mind and heart was already on that plane, and I was intent in following it up with my body. As far as I was concerned, my work was done here, and his was probably really just beginning.

The countryside seemed to take on an even more beautiful and colorful look. It probably had something to do with leaving it, and possibly never seeing it again. On sunny days, in Vietnam, the sky had a blue color unmatched by any other place that I had seen, back in the states. The numerous photographs that I had taken in the course of the year, fortunately, evidence this. It may have had to do with the absence of industrial pollutants and big city smog. We, as Americans probably made great strides in compensating for that. Fortunately, we never succeeded. It was a beautiful country. Without a war here, it would be a great place to visit, and a very worthwhile addition to any tour to the Far East. When I left there, the last thing on my mind was coming back some day, but I'd gladly take the opportunity to do so, and spend some time there, as a civilian. I will return, someday. I don't know when or how, but it will happen.

We arrived at Ben Hoa about eleven o'clock. We made it there with about an hour to spare. All packed, dressed, and ready to go we sat in the terminal, anxious for the word that we had been waiting for all year. It was dream-like. Some of these returnees had vowed to kiss the ground, when they arrived back in the states. I decided to hold out for better things.

As mid-day approached, our instructions were to wait for our names to be read from the flight roster. The long wait was almost over. As our names were read, we proceeded, as a group to the terminal gate. The plane was a big, beautiful DC-8, the most beautiful plane that I had ever seen- for obvious reasons; and it was waiting for us. As our names were checked off at the gate, the only thing left to do was to board the plane. On my turn, I ran all the way up the gangplank, and into the plane. I never looked back.

In less than a half-hour, we were all on board, and ready to go. Our departure from here was in direct contrast to when we arrived. The weather was bright and beautiful, out there. In here, spirits were high, and the excitement was still building, with each step to getting the plane ready for take-off. There were cheers from all of us, when the plane rolled away from the terminal and the excitement reached a new level, as we taxied down the runway. This still seemed unreal.

As the wheels left the ground, all of us erupted with wild cheers, shouts, and long, loud applause for everyone and everything that made this moment possible. Amid this merry-making there were periodic lapses into quiet moments, as all of us took in this very special feeling. We all had our own personal celebration. We were finally on our way home. The feeling was beautiful, the happiness stemming from the most basic of emotions. We were all being taken back- to what, we couldn't be sure; but, at that particular time, it didn't matter.

EPILOGUE

It has been forty-nine years, since I returned to this country, from my tour of duty in Vietnam. For me, as for all of us who were involved, on any given side of the issue, it was a powerful experience. I can really just speak for myself, and of what I had observed. Many other accounts, unfortunately, may never be heard. In completing this work, I should also dedicate it to those who otherwise, for one reason or another, wouldn't be heard. We were there. We didn't have to be shot at, mortared or continually see the war as one shocking experience after another, until it isn't felt anymore. Whether it was on film, a jolting expose' or just in our personal experience- we were there, and we felt it all.

We felt the pain of separation from the ones that we loved. We faced the uncertainty of being put into a situation in which, we were faced with the fear of the possibility of instant death. We experienced joy, in the midst of some of the worst possible situations, on the faces of the Vietnamese children, grateful for the most basic things, like being with their parents. We were made to feel that it wasn't so long ago that we could run to our parents, and they could make everything all right again. Some of us experienced the empty feeling of a missing a friend that we would never see again. (This happened to me even before I left.)

For the ones that returned home, there was the elation of leaving the war behind, as well as sadness for the people that we left there, both living and dead. We also experienced the bewilderment and the hurt of finding out that we had returned home to a world that had changed in its attitude toward this war- too late do us much good- so much so, that we were perceived as part of the problem. We were painful reminders that our country right or wrong had made a mistake and we would all be paying for it for a long time, in many ways. No one has more of a reason to hate war than the people who were sent to fight it.

Some of the most moving moments that I experienced have been when I was honored either as part of the group or as an individual for my being there. I couldn't be present, and it pained me to not be there, for the dedication of the Vietnam Veterans' memorial, in Washington and the burial of the Unknown Soldier from the Vietnam War in Arlington National Cemetery.

I was, however, present for the groundbreaking and dedication of the Maryland Vietnam Veterans' Memorial. Construction of the memorial on Federal Hill was protested by neighborhood residents, after the groundbreaking, who didn't want people "crying on *their* hill." These residents just happened to be some of the people who stayed behind protesting the war and bad-mouthing their country. These were also the same people who flew flags during the Gulf War in support of their gas prices not going up.

Whenever it happened, I was very moved that we were all remembered. I still feel, at times, that it was too little, too late, but I'd have been grateful, even if it were just for the ones who didn't come back.

The reactions to my return were not as enthusiastic as I had envisioned. Individuals who I encountered seemed relatively uninformed and had already ingrained negative opinions about our involvement there. I wasn't mobbed or meticulously questioned about my experience. I was, for the most part, shunned. I was just someone who had returned to the old neighborhood. I could just as well have been in jail to get the same reaction. Whenever I tried to talk about some of the things that happened to me, in Vietnam, and what being there was like, I got blank stares, and answers like "That's nice". I couldn't really say anything without coming up against some negative reaction that depicted American participants in the war as the bad guys, shooting up the landscape and the people, and being involved in a shooting war twenty-four hours a day. The North Vietnamese and the VC were the ones who should have been supported, as far as they were concerned.

I felt that the media was an important factor in that attitude. After so many years of seeing the war on television, it dulled the sensitivities of the viewers at home; eventually it all looked the same.

My experience impressed me even more of how we were looked-upon by our fellow countrymen. It seems to bear repeating that someone, who was there, such as me, was perceived as less of a viable source than that Baltimore Sun editorialist, who probably never left Maryland- let alone Vietnam. Local writers playing to the crowd were much more revered than the actual participants. Some of these writers were so detached that reporting on what really happened would have gotten in the way of their jobs. No one could tell these people anything about the war, and it was perceived that no one, including anyone who had been there, could tell them anything that they didn't already know about the war- except how to end it.

Vietnamese, as far as most Americans were concerned, were relegated to a place in the American consciousness that made them

A Contradiction of Terms: A 25th Division Analyst's Tour in Vietnam

fictional entities that only existed on television, and not part of their real world. Most of the people that I talked to had never met a Vietnamese, from the North or South. Regardless of sides, it seemed to be ignored that these were real people with their existences at stake.

Most people that I tried to talk to were almost unaware that there was a war going on and were just glad not to be personally involved. The only time this view changed was if a brother or husband or friend was wounded, or didn't come back, because of the war- and then it was too real to handle.

Along the way, there were a number of subtle reminders to show us that were not welcomed back or even trusted. The stereotype of a typical returnee, of a person enmeshed in a war, unable to adapt, was even at this early juncture, re-enforced to the point that there was nothing that could be done or said to change these perceptions. I was, obviously unaware of this at first, but eventually the message sunk in. After passing it off, it eventually began to wear on me.

At first, the euphoria of just being back in the country carried me through some of the more difficult confrontations. I could usually cancel out any of the negative reactions that I was subjected to, because of my experience- I was there and they weren't. Adapting one of the sayings that was used a lot over there, I didn't sweat the small stuff- and a lot of it was small stuff- pettiness. What I couldn't see coming was the collective damage the prevailing attitude had on me.

I got my first exposure to this as early as the first leg of the flight, on way to Japan. Before I left, I stocked up on some candy, because I didn't know how soon they were going to feed us. I bought a couple of bags of M&M's, for use at an appropriate time.

About an hour into the flight, I felt a little hungry, and took out one of the bags of candy, and offered it around, just as a stewardess was coming by. We spotted each other at the same time. Seeing the first American women not in a military uniform, in almost a year, I wondered what the first words out of her mouth would sound like, and how she would smile. That, in itself, would have been a nice welcome home. However; when she came up to me, she looked at me, horrified, and demanded to know what I had in my hand. I showed her the candy and offered her some. I was stunned, as she just settled down, and walked away.

I wasn't sure, at first, what had happened; but, as I was asking the question, it dawned on me that she thought that they were pills of some sort. Apparently, this was one of the things that she was supposed to watch out for. I was taken by surprise at her reaction to me, and I was more than a little bit hurt. It was a rather emotionally scarring experience. I put so much personal stock in staying out of that sort of trouble; but she couldn't know that. She apparently had to rely on what she had been warned about. I wanted to talk to her, but she avoided coming by again. As with many things related to the Vietnam experience, it had to remain undone.

When Betty and I first went hunting for an apartment, I found what I thought was a place close to Fort Holabird. Willow Springs Apartments was located just across Dundalk Avenue, opposite the Fort. On the phone, they sounded positive, and I was so convinced that we packed our belongings in my father's station wagon, and came ready to move in. The proprietors of these apartments were counter-culture types, who were apparently intimidated by my short hair and ready admission that I was in the Army, stationed at Holabird. It was also quite possible that their stunned manners may not have been naturally induced.

Almost immediately, they made excuses that they had been up all night, with the police and fire departments, because a tenant had burned herself to death, and they also had to clean up the apartment- which was probably something that the rarely did in their own habitat. This couple had a lackadaisical manner, which seemed devoid of concern for that deceased person, and made us wonder about our own safety. We were both relieved to get out of there. It was difficult to know if these people were for real or not. They did exude a certain detachment from the real world that wasn't really conducive to my idea of a home life. We took our belongings, and moved back to my room, on Furrow Street.

Another attempt, with my father, to check out another Apartment building, produced another small cast of characters, who could have easily fit into an Alfred Hitchcock movie. After that, I abandoned the idea of living around Fort Holabird.

Finally, after checking the register of apartments, which was located at Fort Holabird, we found a place at 360 S. Folcroft Street, about two miles from the fort. It was in a quiet neighborhood. The owners, Joseph and Marietta D'Amico, were very friendly and accommodating, and understood the problems of finding a decent place to live, while in the military. We were always on good terms with them, and our neighbors, and left it with great reluctance, in August of 1973, to return to West Baltimore.

One of the first things that I had promised myself was that, when I returned home, was that I'd buy an air conditioner. We applied for credit, in the old neighborhood, at a place that my parents had dealt with, for a long time. With my impending promotion to E5, I saw no problem in being able to afford it. Credit was refused, on the premise that I was still in the Army, and was, therefore, a poor credit risk. I knew the manager of the store, for a number of years, because my parents had dealt with him. In this case, however, he was very sarcastic, and didn't care to know that I lived around there and wasn't about to be transferred. He acted as if he didn't know me. We did find a store, on the East Side, through some relatives. We never dealt with that store again. In my vocabulary, Ash Sales became "Trash Sales."

These incidents dulled my enthusiasm for being home, and tended to make me rather gun-shy, in dealing with people, when my military background had some bearing on the outcome of the exchange. It was as if I was supposed to hide the fact that I had ever participated at all with the military; and that it was supposed to be something that I was supposed to be ashamed of. I noticed, for instance, that no one else in my unit wore their uniform, off post, unless they had to.

As with all experiences, such as this, it seems appropriate that some of the simplest gestures are best remembered and most effective. It happened to me, shortly after I returned, being stationed at Fort Holabird. I was walking home, after my workday was finished. Not too far from the fort, I approached an elderly couple, walking the opposite way. I was in uniform, and they smiled at me, and stopped me to ask if I had been to Vietnam. They told me that they were aware of all the bad reactions that men returning from there had experienced; and they just wanted to thank me for being there. I didn't really know what to say- except to thank them. Before that moment, I'm not sure that I had heard those words from anyone. If they did, it was without any real meaning. I'll never forget them. It was what they didn't say that gave me the answer to what I was looking for. God bless and keep them. They let me know that I was really home.

A Contradiction of Terms: A 25th Division Analyst's Tour in Vietnam

My Father

On the homefront there were situations that took their toll

My Joseph C, Maguire, Sr. was very proud of this country, the flag and the service and there was never any equivocation about that. I remember him reading things aloud in the 50's and 60's about the Cold War and our involvement during Berlin, Cuban missile crisis and our country's response of the military in these crises, including Vietnam. World War II shaped his opinions and his observations and helped to shape mine about the responsibilities that we all have being Americans. He had his own opinions on Vietnam and we might have differed as to solutions but his support of anything America was involved in with its military was total.

One example of this was when I returned from my tour, my brother Patrick was involved with the Maryland Naval Militia, based on the Frigate *Constellation*, in Baltimore's Inner Harbor. This unit had an interesting mix of characters, which included at least several marines; who put the teenage recruits through drill and ceremony, military discipline among other things. They also regaled the boys with war stories of Vietnam how they survived it by being marines. As a returning veteran, I made it a point to talk to other Vietnam veterans about where they were in Vietnam and when. I had a pretty good sense of what unit was where, and in talking to these creatures was put off with vague answers- ("Which tour?" or "I guess you never walked the point!") It turned out that they were lucky to survive boot camp at Parris Island and to have escaped with their lives from there. They eventually caught in some sort of legal trouble; it had something to do with fraud. My father believed them- right up to the time, they essentially admitted that they were the phonies that they were. Their stories apparently had more appeal than what I was trying to tell him. I was not inclined to misrepresent my involvement. I think It was embarrassing for him. My attitude was that he would just have to get over my not capturing a regiment of VC in my pajamas (Grouch Marx style, in *Animal Crackers:* "I once shot an elephant in my pajamas- how he got there, I'll never know") or not being shot at or killed in Vietnam. We both eventually leveled off and the matter wasn't brought up again. I was, admittedly, very hurt. We both had to rationalize in our own ways that we did what we could in our respective situations and I felt that I had nothing to be ashamed of, at the time, except the people back home. My initial impressions of the days when I first returned were negative. My reactions and theirs were rather unvarnished. I had a long way to go in coming to terms with this.

My father, in one of his letters to me had mentioned that he had written to my commanding officer. Thinking that I would have to be dead for him to get one of those, I asked my company commander, Major Fitzgerald, about it. He didn't seem to remember sending anything like that. I did not think about that until years later.

My father died in April of 1994. When we were going through his papers, among the things that I found was a typed letter in an envelope on White House stationary signed by President Nixon. He answered my father's letter, which apparently expressed support for the war at a time when Nixon really needed it. Case solved!

Vietnam Seminar, University of Baltimore, 1994

To understand what was going at this event more fully it would be best to understand the composition of the audience. This was a cross section unlike any other and it is worth the time and space to try to describe it.

Throughout the audience, these cross-sections were evident. These were very defining events in which General William Westmorland had involved himself in his career, and my feeling was that although he had apparently weathered the worst of the criticism, he was out there to stand up for some more. It was to his credit that he took these opportunities to go before the public and talk about things that years before many would just as well preferred him to just go away, like the many who were under him.

He was the symbol of an involvement gone wrong. There were others; but as a career military man his duty was to uphold the policies of his country. His was one of the more visible positions of policy makers and policy enforcers and in such a position there was no place to hide or to make excuses. The public never took much notice of the individuals who brokered this trouble; they often never do. These are the people who take the flack for the honor of serving their country. On this day he was out there, and he did alright.

Bob Bruger (From Maryland Historical Society) told me about the seminar in the first place; but had declined to attend. In describing his experiences, he was always vague and never really wanted to talk about it. Apparently, as a junior marine officer, he was involved in the siege of Kaison, in 1968. From what I could piece together either he or officers of his type had refused to do some of the duties that were involved in this operation. If this were so, than this would have been a perfect time for him to be there, but he wasn't.

When I heard about the seminar, I called Gary Justice, who was an infantryman at the time. He in turn had told some friends who had some strong opinions as to what generally went on and I had expected some fireworks when these various factions came together.

One standout in this gathering one of my mentors, Tom Jacklin, was there. In my time at the University of Baltimore, I had attended a number of his classes and had learned a great deal about history, research, and the world in general. He was always very candid and forthright and I saw him as, if not the perfect medium to discuss views on Vietnam, at least he served to teach me to put it into the context of other things that were going on at the time. My understanding was that during the Vietnam War, he was out there as one of the people who stood against the war. I had heard and talked to others who did not impress me at all; but this guy was real. My previous experience was of individuals who chanted peace slogans and flaunted their disrespect for this country. Tom's appeal was that he, in effect, said that although he opposed the policies, he was still a citizen and it was his country too. He taught me that you can disagree in this society and still be part of it. Vilification is a constant. Expect to be disagreed with; but it is up to us to learn from what's going on in the country and make the most of it. If there is a book to write or a political agenda to follow, it is up to us to educate ourselves about everything that is going on, to do the best job possible. Over the years we may have grown apart, but I will never forget the focus that he provided me in my development as an interpreter of ongoing events. Tom was there and this coming together was complete.

Bibliographies

These were sources gathered in the making of this project. Although this is an essentially a personal account, there were numerous instances in which facts were checked and assessments made from various archival and book sources.
General conclusions were reached in the use of this material were reached and no specific references were used at this point for in-text references.

Bibliographic Sources: National Archives

In the time elapsed since the gathering of the archival sources, some of this material may be located in a different National Archives facility and updates are in order.

OVERVIEW OF RELEVANT RECORD GROUPS FOR
25TH DIVISION
FROM 1970 AND 1971
LOCATED AT NARS ANNEX, SUITLAND, MARYLAND

FROM SUMMARY NOTES MADE ON 9 MAY 1988

25th Division information office
    Press releases

J. C. Maguire Jr.

338-81-327 -89015

        8 March to April 1970
        9 April to May 1970
        10 May to June 1970
        11 June to July 1970
        12 July to August 1970
        13 August 1970
        14 Aug. to Sept. 1970
        15 Sept. to Nov. 1970

338-85-1599

        # 1 biographical file
        Tropic Lightning News- oversize

25th Division G2 Daily Journal

338-81-301

NA Box No. 22	1 Feb to 30 April 1970
23	1 May to 30 July 1970
24	1 Aug to 26 November 1970

INTSUMS

338-81-302

NA Box No. 12	1 January to 15 March 1970
13	16 March to 31 May 1970
14	1 June to 15 August 1970
15	16 Aug to 17 November 1970

25th Division G2- Ranger Taking Orders

338-81-303
> 70-1 to 70-89 July to October 1970

PERINTREPS- 25th Division G2 Command Reports

338-81-310
- PW/HC Exploitation Reports
- PW Status Reports
- Measurements of Progress Reports
- Volunteer Information Program Reports
- VC/NVA Base [ill] Neutralization Reports
- Operations against Local Forces
- Control, Turn-in and Disposal of Captured Enemy Weapons
- Intelligence Collection Plan
- Cambodia (Gunboat Reports)
- Transmission Security Reports

25th Division G3 Journal

338-81-308

NA Box	Dates
31	January 1969 to 15 January 1970
32	16 January to 15 February 1970
33	16 February to 20 March 1970
34	21 March to 20 April 1970
35	21 April to 25 May 1970
36	26 May to 30 June 1970
37	1 July to 31 July 1970
38	1 August to 25 August 1970

J. C. Maguire Jr.

39	26 August to 25 September 1970
40	26 September to 25 October 1970
26	October to 18 November 1970

25th Division G3 After-Action Reports

NA Box No. 1 Cambodian Operations, 1970
    Wheeler Place, 1969
    [ill], 1968
    Yellowstone, 1968

25th Division SIP REPS

338-81-312
    NA Box No.1 Cambodian Border Incidents, April 1968

338-81-361   Operational Ops Study, 1970
                      Summary of Support Activities (G5)

338-81-367
    NA Box No. 2 Maneuver Units OpSUM- 70

25th Division DISCOM Chaplain Daily Journal

338-81-392
    NA Box No. 1 13 February to 22 November 1970

25th Division 1st Brigade History

338-81-331
    NA Box No. 1 Annual History Supplements, 1968-69

25th Division [First Brigade]

338-81-336
    NA Box No. 7 S2 Daily Journal 1 August to 9 August 1970
    " 14   S3 Daily Journal 14 January to 31 May 1970
    " 15   1 June to 15 August 1970
    " 16 "   16 August to 10 October 1970
    " 17 "   11 October to15 November 1970

25th Division 1st Brigade After-Action Reports

338-81-339
    NA Box No. 1   Operation Cliff Dweller, 1968
                        Toan Thang, 1969
                        Attack on Nui Ba Den, 1969
                        Operation Bold Lancer I, 1970
                        Operation Bold Lancer II, 1970

25th Division 1st Brigade Sit REPS

338-81-339
    NA Box No. 2 October 1969 to November 1970

25th Division Sequence of Event Reports

338081-337
    NA Box NO. 1 4 March to 3 November 1970

25th Division 2nd Brigade S2/S3 Daily Journal

338-81-422
    NA Box No. 21   1 January to 10 February 1970

J. C. Maguire Jr.

	22	11 February to 20 April 1970
	23	21 April to June 1970
	24	1 July to 10 September 1970
	25	11 September to 20 November 1970
	26	21 November to 31 December 1970

338-81-423

	26	1 January 20 January 1971
	27	21 January to 5 April 1971

25th Division 2nd Brigade S2 INTSUMS

338-81-424
    NA Box   5 January to September 1970
                           6 October 1970 to March 1971

25th Division Ranger Tasking Orders

338-81-425
    NA Box No. 1   [ill] 70-1 [to] 70-12
                           71-1 [to] [1-28-71]

25th Division 2nd Brigade OPS Reports

338-81-426
Command Reports-
    NA Box No. 1 M-1968 to Feb 1971
        After-Action Reports 66-69
                4 1 January to 30 April 1970
                5 1 May 31 December 1970
                1 January to 3 April 1970

Weekly Briefing Reports   70-71
Monthly
Command Ops

25 Division Base Camp Defense

338-81-377
    3 Boxes Daily Journal 3 boxes], January to December 1969

338-81-301
    Press Releases were incomplete and not in order
    Daily Journal, During February to July 1970 Spot reports on PW's and Returnees
    Interrogation Reports and Translations of Captured Enemy Documents

TOC Daily Journal

338-82-[548-366] combined with G3 Air and Camp defense Journal

Bibliographic Sources- Books

Bloodworth, Dennis, An Eye for the Dragon: Southeast Asia, Observed: 1954-1970. New York: Farrar, Straus and Giroux, 1970.

Bloodworth, Dennis. The Chinese Looking Glass, New York: Farrar, Straus and Giroux, 1967.

Buell, Hal. Vietnam: Land of Many Dragons. New York: Dodd, Meade & Company, 1968.

Committee of Concerned Asian Scholars. The Indochina Story: A Fully Documented Account. New York: Pantheon Books, 1970.

Dawson, Alan. 55 Days: The Fall of South Vietnam. Englewood Cliffs, N.J: Prentice- Hall, 1977.

Denton, Senator Jeremiah A., Jr. When Hell Was in Session. Mobile: Traditional Press, 1982.

Ehrhart, William D. Vietnam-Perkasie: A Combat Marine Memoir. United States: McFarland, 1983. [315p.]

Ehrhart, William D. Marking Time. New York: Avon Books, 1986. [296p.]

Gordon, Bernard K. The Dimensions of the Conflict in Southeast Asia: Englewood Cliffs [NJ]: Prentice Hall, 1966.

Hope, Bob, with Melville Shavelson. Don't Shoot, It's Only Me: Bob Hope's Comedy History of the United States. New York: Putnam, 1990.

Hope, Bob. Bob Hope's Vietnam Story: Five Women I Love. Garden City, New York: Doubleday & Company, 1966.

Johnson, Lyndon Baines .The Vantage Point. New York: Holt, Rhinehart and Winston, 1971.

Kennan, George F. Memoirs: 1950-1963. Boston: Little, Brown & Company, 1972.

Kissinger, Henry A. White House Years. Boston: Little, Brown & Company, 1979.

Lacouture, Jean. Vietnam: Between Two Truces. New York: Random House, 1966.

Leader, William J. and Eugene Burdick. The Ugly American. New York: W. W. Norton, 1958.

Mangold, Tom, and John Pennycate. The Tunnels of Cu Chi. New York: Random House, 1985.

Marshall, S.L.A. Ambush: The Story of Dau Tieng. New York: Cowles Book Company, Inc., 1969.

McJunkin, James N. and Max D. Grace. Visions of Vietnam. Novato [CA]: Presidio Press, 1983.

McNamara, Robert S. The Essence of Security: Reflections in Office. New York: Harper & Row, 1968.

McNamara, Robert S. In Retrospect: The Tragedy and Lessons of Vietnam. New York: Times Books, Random House, 1995.

Michener, James A. Kent State: What Happened and Why .New York: Random House, 1971.

Nixon, Richard M., No More Vietnams. New York: Arbor House, 1985.

Nixon, Richard M. The Memoirs of Richard Nixon. New York: Touchtone, Simon and Schuster, 1990.

O'Neill, Thomas P., Jr., with William Novak. Man of the House: The Life and Political Memiors of Speaker Tip O'Neill. New York: Random House, 1987.

Parks, David. G.I. Diary. Washington, D.C.: Howard University Press, 1968.

Parrish, John A. 12, 20 & 5: A Doctor's Year in Vietnam. New York: E. P. Dutton, 1972.

Schlesinger, Arthur M., Jr. A Thousand Days: John F. Kennedy in the White House. Boston: Houghton Mifflin Company, 1965.

Schlesinger, Arthur M., Jr. The Bitter Heritage: Vietnam and American Democracy: 1941-1966. Boston: Houghton Mifflin, 1966.

Sheehan, Neil, Hedrick Smith, E. W. Kenworthy and Fox Butterfield. The Pentagon Papers. New York: Bantam Books, 1971.

Sorensen, Theodore C., Kennedy. New York: Harper & Row, 1965.

Stanton, Shelby. Vietnam Order of Battle. New York: Galahad Books, 1986.

Index

"F Troop",. See Company F
1st Air Cavalry, 61, 62
25th Division, 49, 51, 61, 62, 92, 97, 98, 101, 141, 144, 176, 177, 178, 179, 180
25th MIC, 35, 51, 52, 54, 61, 76, 77, 85, 86, 89, 99, 102, 111, 117, 138, 140, 152, 154, 155, 159
25TH MIC, 51
5th NVA Division, 62
70-RA-2., 39
7th NVA Division, 62
9th NVA Division, 62
AFVN (Armed Forces Rado Network, 67
Aggressor, 35
Air Force, 14, 16, 17, 21, 42, 85, 127
Apollo XIII, 41, 42, 44
Arlington National Cemetery, 19, 20, 169
Army, 19, 21, 22, 23, 27, 28, 29, 30, 31, 32, 33, 34, 35, 37, 39, 41, 45, 46, 50, 52, 54, 65, 76, 86, 91, 98, 100, 102, 111, 127, 145, 149, 162, 163, 171, 172
ARVN (Army, Republic of Vietnam, 56, 64, 71, 76, 98, 102, 130, 131, 141
Ba Cau, 58

Ba Hai, 83
Baltimore, 14, 26, 27, 42, 45, 50, 56, 63, 69, 73, 88, 90, 96, 123, 124, 125, 172
Bardsley, Rodney, 14
Barker, Roger, 52, 67, 86, 109
Ben Hoa, 44, 45, 48, 49, 167
Boi Loi Woods, 61
Bon Secours Hospital, 17, 40, 98
Brennan, Father Sylvan, 40
Brown, First Sgt., 29, 31, 54, 108, 111, 154, 165, 182
Bryant, Sharon, 15, 16
Bunker guard, 73, 78, 81
C-121, 48
Cambodia, 62, 63, 79, 99, 131, 141, 177
Camp Frenzel Jones, 68, 102, 103, 122
Captain Debolt, 54, 63
Chinook helicopter, 79
Collins, Rick, 69
Company F, 27
Cook, First Sgt., 52, 83
Cu Chi, 35, 45, 48, 49, 51, 57, 58, 67, 68, 75, 77, 79, 85, 87, 88, 91, 92, 94, 96, 98, 99, 100, 101, 102, 103, 105, 106, 108, 110, 112, 113, 115, 122, 127, 154, 156, 163, 182
D'Alasandro, Mayor Thomas, III, 69

267

Dau Tieng, 61, 62, 79, 182
Declaration of Independence, 18
DMZ, 14
Dundalk, 171
Edwards, Sheila, 19, 20
Evans, 24
Fort Bragg, 22, 23, 26, 28, 32, 36
Fort Bragg., 22, 26, 28, 32
Fort Holabird, 21, 26, 27, 28, 29, 34, 43, 58, 61, 70, 85, 100, 108, 127, 159, 161, 171, 172
Fort Myer, 20
French, 52, 59, 104, 122, 132
Friendship Airport, 41
Gabriel, Sgt., 30, 31, 32, 33
Gaither, Mr., 52
Garcia, Benny, 51, 69, 70
Gonzales, 24
Green, Eddie, 52, 88
Gruntnamese, 52
Guam, 43, 44, 58
Hai, Ba, 82
Harker, "Gunny", 35, 36, 37, 109
Hawaii, 43, 87, 97, 164
Headquarters Company, 68, 76, 78, 93, 97, 127, 151
Hedrick, Ray, 28
Hill, Al, 52, 67, 87
Ho Bo Woods, 61
Holabird. See Fort Holabird, See Fort Holabird, See Fort Holabird, See Fort Holabird, See Fort Holabird, See Fort Holabird, See Fort Holabird, See Fort Holabird, See Fort Holabird, See Fort Holabird, See Fort Holabird, See Fort Holabird, See Fort Holabird, See Fort Holabird, See Fort Holabird
III Corps, 57, 58
Iron Triangle, 61, 62
Irving, Sgt. "Red", 22
Jessie, 55, 76
Kahn, Sgt., 56, 130
Kent State, 64, 79, 182
Kontom, 63
Korea, 35, 49, 144
Korean War, 12, 77, 119
Krocynski, 25
Lei, Hia Hung, 15, 16, 82, 83
Lind, Ray, 69
Little, Lorenzo, 24
Long Binh, 46, 49, 58, 68, 98, 102, 103, 104, 111, 121, 122, 125, 128, 129, 130, 131, 132, 136, 137, 139, 140, 143, 147, 148, 151, 152, 156, 159
M.A.S.H, 12
Macrael, Jim, 88
Macrail, Jim, 51
MACV J2, 63
Maguire, Betty, 9, 21, 25, 27, 39, 40, 56, 70, 74, 94, 97, 98, 153, 171
Maguire, Joseph B., Jr., 39, 40, 94, 95, 96, 121
Maguire, Linda, 39, 97
Maguire, Patrick Michael, 69
Manago, 25
marines, 29, 33, 39
Marines, 14, 21, 28, 29, 30, 31, 32, 33
Marshall Atoll, 44
Maryland Historical Society, iv
McAllister, C. J., 24
McGovern, Senator George, 65
Mekong River, 49, 57, 61, 94

Melendez, Julio, 25
Michalic, First Sgt. George, 54
Michelon Rubber Plantation, 61
monsoons, 73
Moog, Larry, 85, 87, 96, 118, 122, 126, 138, 154, 155, 165
Mui Tan, 82, 83, 84
National Archives, 62, 92, 100, 118
National Guard, 21, 32, 64
National Liberation Front, 37
Neimeyer, David, 89
Neimyer, David, 70, 108, 118, 126, 139, 154
Newhart, 25
Nixon , Richard, 182
Nixon, Richard, 18, 63, 64, 117, 182
NLF. See National Liberation Front
Nol, Lon, 62, 63
North Vietnamese, 36, 57, 59, 61, 62, 65, 79, 133, 135, 136, 166, 170
North, Oliver, 36
North, Virginia, iii
Nui Ba Den, 61, 62, 79, 179
NVA, 57, 59, 61, 62, 63, 64, 99, 104, 114, 117, 130, 135, 136, 141, 142, 159, 177
Oakland, 39, 41, 42, 166, 167
OB shop, 54, 61, 63, 67, 76, 77, 78, 87, 96, 97, 106, 126, 140, 141, 152
Odette, Larry, 56
Oler, Ned, 25
Parker, 25
Pentagon, 20, 183
Perry, Mr., 54, 90
Petrecho, 24, 25
Philippines, 44
Phoenix, 34
PJohnson, President Lyndon, 36

Pleku, 58
reserve, 32
Richie, Major, 35
Roberts, First Sgt., 24
Runnels, Al, 52
Runnels, John, 67, 87
Rusty, 55
Saigon, 15, 16, 45, 49, 57, 58, 63, 64, 68, 79, 97, 103, 104, 106, 121, 122, 123, 124, 126, 132, 156
Saigon., 49, 57, 122, 123
San Francisco, 41, 167
Scaruzzi, Mike, 52, 87
Schroeder, Noel, 56, 71
Sciukas, Victor "Butch", 28
Shepard, Shepard, 54
Smith,, 50
Sneed, Joe, 67, 96
St. Benedict, 28
St. Benedict's, 29
Stars and Stripes, 44, 161
Sun Papers, 10
Svay Rieng, 63
Tactical Operations Center (TOC), 61
Tay Ninh, 49, 61, 62
Trans-International Airlines, 42
Travis Air Force Base, 42, 85, 127, 166
Tropic Lightning News, 61, 176
Tuder, Albert, 40
University in Quebec, 15
University of Baltimore, 17, 63
VC, 34, 35, 59, 61, 62, 64, 83, 99, 104, 114, 115, 117, 129, 130, 135, 141, 142, 147, 148, 159, 170, 177
Viet Cong, 36, 57, 59, 61, 135, 166

Vietnam, iv, 9, 10, 12, 14, 15, 16, 20, 21, 27, 28, 32, 35, 36, 37, 38, 39, 41, 42, 43, 44, 45, 48, 49, 50, 51, 52, 54, 57, 58, 63, 64, 65, 69, 71, 85, 88, 91, 95, 96, 98, 100, 102, 103, 107, 108, 114, 115, 119, 121, 127, 131, 132, 133, 134, 136, 139, 144, 145, 148, 149, 156, 158, 163, 165, 166, 167, 169, 170, 171, 173, 181, 182, 183

Vietnamese, 9, 10, 15, 16, 36, 37, 38, 45, 46, 52, 53, 58, 61, 62, 64, 68, 75, 76, 77, 82, 83, 84, 91, 97, 98, 99, 102, 104, 108, 112, 115, 116, 117, 118, 122, 123, 124, 125, 127, 128, 130, 131, 132, 133, 134, 135, 137, 139, 140, 143, 144, 145, 146, 147, 148, 149, 151, 156, 159, 162, 166, 169, 170

War, Glenn, 69

Washington, 12, 18, 19, 20, 38, 169, 182

White House, 18, 19, 182

World War II, 19, 35

Xuan Loc, 68, 70, 76, 84, 85, 86, 89, 91, 92, 94, 97, 98, 99, 102, 103, 104, 105, 106, 107, 108, 109, 110, 111, 112, 115, 116, 117, 118, 119, 120, 122, 125, 127, 128, 129, 130, 131, 132, 136, 137, 138, 139, 141, 144, 145, 146, 147, 148, 151, 152, 154, 155, 156, 157, 164

Made in the USA
Middletown, DE
02 November 2021